Pardon My
BACKCAST

Alan Pratt

with illustrations by the author

A *Frank* **mato**

PORTLAND

Dedication

To the Echo chainsaw people, who provided the means whereby Wilma, my current wife of 44 years, could cut the firewood necessary to keep my workroom warmed to a proper book-writing temperature.

To the University of Pinole, which bestowed upon me a degree in Pedomancy, which has greatly improved my acne, punctuation, and the content, if not the quality, of this volume.

To Milford "Stanley" Poltroon, whose incomparable hearty breakfast recipe, POOT (Poltroon's Original Oat Treat), afforded the nutrients vital to countering "writers' lag," plus more Riboflavin than I could possibly use daily.

And to all those fishing companions, who gave so freely of advice and counsel, flies and wader patches, beer and wine, and otherwise failed utterly to discourage me from perpetrating this tome: Steve, Dick, Bob, Jerry, Ed, John, Walt, Fred, Bill, Stan, Cal, Gordy and Jean, Boyd and Bea, Jim and Carol, Lewis and Clark and, of course, Mark and Ben.

Published in 1996 by Frank Amato Publications, Inc.
(503) 653-8108

Illustrations: Alan Pratt
Book design and Layout: Tony Amato
Softbound ISBN: 1-57188-059-3   UPC: 0-66066-00251-8

1 3 5 7 9 10 8 6 4 2

PRINTED IN CANADA

THIS BOOK

has been sanitized for your protection, but should not be taken internally except with parental guidance, permission of your parole officer or under supervision of a physician.

Contents

Introduction 6
Foreword 10
Introduction to Culture 11
Do You Have a Brain ? 12
Piscatorial Pachyderms 13
The Highly Regarded Double-Haul Cast . . . 14
The Great Fly Fishing Fraud 15
An Entire Chapter Devoted to Getting Lost . . . 16
Lefty 19
More about Casting 21
The Esthetic Appeal of Fly Casting 22
A Fly Fisher's Ten Commandments 23
Creative Wading, Part MXIIV 25
Creative Wading, Part CLXVI 26
General Procedures for Successfully Falling in . . . 27
A Word about Adhesives 28
How to Find West Yellowstone 29
Fishbooks 32
Great Fish Reading 33
A Gold Mine 34
Identifying Trout Made Easy 34
Reading the Water 36
How to See Fish 37
Choosing a Fly Rod 38
Shamans Make Sense 40
We Regret 41
Food for Fly Fishers 42
Image of the Fly Fisher 43
Appropriate Dress 43
Tackle and Gear 45
Say it with a Sneer 45
Communicating with Words and Phrases . . . 45
Think Kindly of the Worm 46
Streamside Etiquette 47
Entering the Water 48
Casting 49

Covering the Rise 49
Wading 49
Do Fish Smell? 49
Springtime = Trout 51
Fishfights 52
Cutthroat Skiffing 53
Thumbs 54
Pike and Walleyes on Flies? 55
Fly Tying 59
Local Fishing 60
The Poltroon Connection 61
Renew Spirits and Solve Global Problems . . . 66
Aphorisms to Fish By 66
Floating Craft 67
Who invented Fly Fishing? 68
Companions 68
Cussing 70
Gramps 70
Fishwagons 72
Fish Gods 74
Missing the Big Chance 75
Thunder and Lightning 76
A Cathartic Expose of Why Fly-Fishing Books Never
      Make the Best-Seller List 76
Worrying 77
Loners 77
Are You Really Ready for Fly Fishing? 78
Epilogue 79

50% OFF

is what Al Pratt has been accused of being by most of his three (3) friends and the 300,000 readers of *The Seattle Times* for whom he cartooned for 41 years. Al's proctologist, Dr. Bill McMahon, says the claim is only half right.

Introduction

There has never been another fly-fishing book quite like this one. That's because this is the only one ever written by Alan Pratt. That's too bad—he should have written more, as you'll agree when you've read this—but at least he blessed us with this single offering.

Who was Alan Pratt? If you were among the legions who knew him, he needs no introduction. If not, then you missed the delightful company of a gentle and funny man who loved rivers and trout and people. He was also a man with a great gift for expressing things in both images and words, talents he combined with a slightly off-center view of the world that allowed him to see humor in all things, especially fly fishing.

Fly fishing was Al's avocation and frequent passion, and for him it was always pure, unrelenting fun. As a lifelong participant in the sport, starting many years before it became popular or trendy, he was well qualified to discuss fly fishing in serious terms, yet he always chose to poke fun at it instead—at its methods, tackle, personalities, terminology, and virtually every other aspect of it.

That's what he has done in this book. In one sense it is a semi-legitimate overview of fly fishing, serving up genuinely useful information along with hearty doses of humor, but it goes well beyond the basics of the sport to consider some elements you will not find discussed anywhere else—such as the use of elephants as off-road vehicles, how to prepare for getting lost, or how to take care of your thumbs. Since the fly-fishing world seems preoccupied with creating and exalting its own celebrities, it's hardly surprising that Al has a little fun at their expense in these pages, too. He also ruminates facetiously upon the origins of the sport, acknowledges its restorative powers and other satisfactions, and offers glimpses of some of his own memorable angling experiences, including pleasant days astream with favorite fishing companions.

So that is the delicious and always funny angling menu served in these pages, a learning and laughing experience that will leave you feeling as if you'd always been a friend of Alan Pratt.

You can read Al's biography, in his own words, at the end of this book. But since he was characteristically modest (and funny) in writing about his own life, it seems appropriate to give a somewhat more detailed account of it here.

Born in Portland, Oregon, Al had two grandfathers who fished—you'll meet them in these pages—which probably meant he was genetically disposed to become a fisherman himself. Taking no chances on that score, his grandfathers saw to it that Al

began fishing at a very early age in the small streams of northwest Oregon and south-west Washington. Perhaps that early introduction to the gentle, contemplative sport of angling helped shape Al's personality, which was also contemplative and gentle.

As a child Al moved with his parents to Seattle, where he quickly busied himself exploring local waters. He graduated from Seattle's Roosevelt High School and attend-ed the University of Washington before being caught up in World War II, during which he served with distinction as an infantry officer in the European Theater.

I happen to know something about his military career because I once heard a detailed account of it. This was in my camper, parked on the shore of Hood Canal where Al and I and Ed Foss had gone to fish for sea-run cutthroat. Al was swapping war stories with Ed, and in the wee hours of the morning, after the consumption of copious quantities of Jack Daniel's, they concluded it was Foss's artillery battery that fired the fateful shell that toppled a German church steeple onto Al's company com-mander, resulting in a battlefield promotion for Al.

After the war Al returned to Seattle to pursue gainful employment and take up fly fishing, not necessarily in that order. Ignoring his father's advice to the contrary, he sought a position as a newspaper artist at *The Seattle Times* where his father was already employed in the same capacity. He was hired as an entry-level editorial artist, which meant his chief duty was retouching photographs. He once described the work in these words: "We wipe the smiles off photos for obituaries, de-wrinkle the elderly, open closed eyes, put neckties on the T-shirted, and de-navel the bathing-suited."

His employment threw him into company with the strange assortment of charac-ters that then inhabited *The Times'* newsroom, including Robert A. Barr, a reporter who fished with flies during occasional moments of sanity, and Enos Bradner, the newspaper's curmudgeonly outdoor editor and founding president of the Washington Fly Fishing Club, one of the oldest and most respected angling organizations in the country. As Al relates in this book, it was through his association with Bradner that he became acquainted with the club. His artistic talents were quickly recognized by the members, who asked him to design an emblem, and he came up with a maroon-and-white shield emblazoned with a fly pattern; club members have been wearing it on their fishing vests and jackets ever since.

Al became a full-fledged member of the club in 1951 and quickly began con-tributing to its affairs in other ways. He furnished illustrations for the club's monthly newsletter, the *Creel Notes*, drew posters publicizing the club's casting and tying classes, designed get-well cards for its ailing members, and made the invitations for its famous Christmas parties.

But invitations were the least of his contributions to the Christmas parties. He also portrayed fabulous characters in Christmas-party skits, most notably the intrepid explorer Sir Archibald Frobisher-Frobisher of the Tottering on the Thames Dry-by-All-Means Fly-Fishing Club. From the inexhaustible depths of his own imagination, he also conjured up a series of incredible awards which he began presenting to the most outrageously deserving club members. These became known as the Goofus Awards, and they included intricate working mechanical devices that Rube Goldberg would have envied, all built from what Al called his "culch pile" of odds and ends (years later, viewing a collection of Goofus Awards, Al's son, Mark, recognized bits and pieces of many of his childhood toys). Over the years Al gradually became THE entertainment at the Fly Fishing Club's Christmas party, and his Goofus awards became a sort of peculiar badge of honor, coveted as much as any of the serious awards given by the club.

Simultaneously Al was also busy forging a notable career. He was promoted to chief cartoonist of *The Seattle Times*, which gave him the opportunity to exercise his artist's pen in many different ways. In addition to the cartoons he regularly drew to illustrate columns, features, or news stories, he began a series called "Prattlings" that was published weekly in *The Times'* Sunday magazine for many years. These cartoons, occupying a full page in the magazine, allowed him to explore many topics, and their great variety of thematic material was a reflection of both the depths of Al's imagination and his humor. He also illustrated fly patterns and drew fishing maps to accompany Bradner's popular column, *The Inside on the Outdoors*, and the elaborate cartoons he drew in annual celebration of opening day of the trout season became popular with anglers and collectors alike.

Al had a special affinity for maps, and if you looked at one he had drawn you always knew it was accurate, mainly because most of his maps were of areas he had personally fished or explored. But he also considered maps a vital aspect of human culture, as demonstrated by the profound question he was fond of asking: "Without maps, where would we be today?"

Once, when asked what it took to be a successful newspaper cartoonist, Al replied: "One must know what an aardvark looks like, how a bulldozer works, how a salmon spawns, what the clad and unclad human anatomy looks like, how to wire a three-way light switch, and have a working knowledge of the Gatling gun, the gopher, and the Stillson wrench."

In addition to his newspaper work he illustrated numerous books on fly fishing, including Bradner's *Northwest Angling*, Lenox Dick's *The Art and Science of Fly Fishing*, Jim Green's *Fly Casting from the Beginning*, Polly Rosborough's *Memoirs from 50 Years of Flyrodding*, the first edition of my own *Kamloops*, and others. He also designed and illustrated *Backcasts*, a book published to commemorate the 50th anniversary of the Washington Fly Fishing Club.

But cartooning was only one of his talents. He also was a gifted writer, publishing articles in *The Flyfisher*, *Angler* magazine, *Flyfishing*, and other periodicals. He was also well known within the angling community for his work on *The Wretched Mess News*, now fondly remembered as an off-the-wall piscatorial publication that sprang from the odd but fertile brain of the late Stanley Bascom, who went under the pseudonym Milford Poltroon. *The Wretched Mess News* pledged to subscribers that it would bring "culture, poise and also fish" to their lives, and while it sometimes may have fallen short of that promise, it never failed to make them laugh.

Al and Milford Poltroon were kindred free spirits, and you will find many references to Milford in these pages. That's only fitting, for of all Al's many angling companions, Milford Poltroon undoubtedly had the greatest influence on his fishing and artistic careers. The two also worked together to create the *Wretched Mess Calendar*, which included a host of strange holidays you couldn't find anywhere else, and the hot-selling calendar became a fixture on desks all the way from the Pentagon to Palm

Springs—until, one year, Al and Milford inadvertently omitted the 28th of July. After that, sales were never quite the same.

The two also collaborated to give history's first (and probably only) fly-tying demonstration over the radio. Just think about that for a moment.

Al was also an innovative fly tier, a talented sculptor and woodworker, a first-rate fishing companion, an artful angler, and a highly entertaining story-teller who always seemed to have exactly the right words for any occasion. When the Washington Fly Fishing Club decided to name an award after Letcher Lambuth, one of its most distinguished founding members, it was Al who designed and made the wooden plaque that became known as the Letcher Lambuth Angling Craftsman Award. Appropriately, in 1991 the award was presented to Al himself for his many contributions to the crafts of angling.

Al was also a devoted family man. With his wife, Wilma, he raised two daughters and a son, enjoyed the company of a whole passel of grandchildren, and lived to see the birth of his first great-grandchild.

After he retired from *The Seattle Times*, he sold his home on Bear Creek northeast of Seattle—once it had been surrounded by woods, but real-estate developers were moving in on all sides, and that was something that Al simply could not abide—and moved to a pleasant location along the western shore of Camano Island, atop a bluff looking out over Saratoga Passage. There, with a fine view of the water, Whidbey Island, and the Olympic Mountains looming to the west, he settled down to work on the scores of projects he always had going—one of which was this book.

So now you know a little about Alan Pratt and the kind of man he was. But no words can ever fully capture the essence of his personality, or the rare quality he had of making people feel cheerful merely by his presence. Uncommonly talented, he was also uncommonly generous with his talents, and he had a spark that most men lack. He was one of a kind, and when he left us it was as if a light had suddenly gone out in the lives of everyone who knew him.

Al died suddenly on March 4, 1994, while traveling in Arizona. This book was still unfinished at the time of his death. His son, Mark, and daughter-in-law, Berlinda, found some parts of the text stored on computer disks and others in longhand notes scattered about Al's cluttered studio on Camano Island. Berlinda graciously volunteered to key the longhand notes onto computer disks; for this work she deserves the greatest thanks.

The Washington Fly Fishing Club decided to sponsor publication of the book as a tribute to Al and his more than 40 years of friendship and service to the club. As his longtime friend and fishing companion, it has been my pleasant task to assemble the book for publication—I hesitate to use the word "edit," for very little editing was required.

I'm glad I had the chance to do this—it was like being in the company of my old friend once again—and I know that if the situation had been reversed, Al would have tried to do the same for me.

Steve Raymond

—*Steve Raymond*
September, 1995

Foreword

Most really great works of literature needed no effusive preamble to render credible the author or his prose. Tolstoy's *War and Peace* didn't need one. Nor did *Decline and Fall of Practically Everybody*, by Cuppy, or *A Farewell to Arms*. Books on fly fishing, however, can use all the help they can get. Especially this one.

The proliferation of fishing books in recent years also has severely depleted the supply of first-rate foreword writers, and the best of them are considerably overworked, to the point where it cuts into their fishing time, and they are not likely to answer the phone if they think it's another aspiring author fishing for a foreword.

Many of the big-time outdoor writers I know, who recognize my non-authoritative position as a fly fisher, were unavailable for one or another good reason, or had other commitments or reservations. Several others, including Lee Wulff and Enos Bradner, managed to become unavailable by expiring. C'est la vie.

Even my favorite non-Nobel Prize-winning author, the late, much-loved Milford ("Stanley") Poltroon, had reservations, over in Tullahoma, Tenn., and expressed reluctance toward having anything to do with the project, saying, "I express reluctance toward having anything to do with the project." Then he up and expired, too.

Thus, to save strain on your attention span, it's probably best that you ignore this foreword and utilize the space for jotting phone numbers or grocery lists or just plain doodling. The remainder of this book is not all that bad, though, and you might as well look at the splendidly illustrative illustrations.

—*Alan Pratt*

Introduction to Culture

Since the advent of the zipper, automatic transmissions and instant coffee, and the resultant downhill slide of our culture, we have been left with scant few exercises calling for skill of hand and mind. This is semi-tragic, in that we may well evolve into a species *(Homo digitus)* marked by recessive brows and hands with but a thumb and single digit, suitable only for poking computer keyboards and opening kiddie-proof pill bottles. Our individual sports may become limited to the likes of falconry, video games or six-meter yacht racing, each involving but a modicum of finesse or thought, but considerable money. Pity!

There is, however, one (1) activity that can lift you out of the muck and mire in which you find yourself today, bring culture once again into your drab life, and reward you with a rejuvenated spirit and new-found ineptitudes: FLY FISHING.

In order to fully enjoy fly fishing I would caution you to approach the sport with a well-ventilated mind, loose clothing and a reasonable checking-account balance. Remember to breathe deeply, using the stomach rather than the diaphragm. Consume only natural foods heavy in fiber, i.e., spinach, shredded wheat, Jack Daniel's. And, above all, do not clutter your mind with needless facts.

It is possible to go through an entire lifetime of three score and ten or 101 years, whichever comes first, without ever learning to fly fish. Many successful people of note have done so without apparent trauma. Ragnar the Stupid, a Celtic chieftain, did not fish, preferring instead to crack skulls and practice other brutalities. Nor did Genghis Khan, who ruled an empire almost entirely devoid of good trout streams. Robert Fulton came near inventing the steam-powered fly reel, but judged it unsuitable for the market of the day. Neither Anhauser nor Busch gave fishing or fishermen much thought, but their legacy, the six-pack, has nurtured fly anglers everywhere.

But the mere fact that others have lived their lives without the benefit of fly fishing is no reason why YOU should do likewise, no. In this century, several presidents (and possibly a dictator or two), plus many rich and famous individuals, have been practicing fly fishers. Naturally you will wish to emulate them.

There are several ways to learn fly fishing, most of them wrong. You can, for instance, be introduced to the sport by:

A. The pre-packaged fishing department of your local super-drug mart.
2. Your Uncle Fred.
III. A book.

Each has the potential for starting you off on the romantic road to fly fishing. Each also has the capacity to throw at you an agglomeration of technical and philosophical information which may overpower any enthusiasm you have for the game.

The tackle salesman at the super-drug mart in most cases probably fishes only with worms, if at all, and would like to sell you some leaders and a jar of salmon eggs and send you on your way.

Uncle Fred likely is possessed of some considerable faulty fishing habits, plus being an atrocious caster.

In books, however, you can find a myriad of techniques and words of wisdom on the ways of fishes and how to overcome certain casting errors.

Yet books also tend to give you the idea that fly fishing—while the only legitimate way to go—is also difficult. Baloney! Potty training is difficult, but you learned that, didn't you? Didn't you?

Books also will tell you that fly fishing is expensive. Baloney again! It's only money; a man cannot live on bread alone.

Furthermore, books will advise you that fly fishing requires great intelligence. Baloney yet one more time! Many successful fly fishers have the IQ of onions.

All right, so this book is full of baloney. If baloney is not to your taste, or you are allergic to it, or if you're absorbed in counting calories, controlling cholesterol, or minimizing flatulence, you had best drop this book and run like hell, for you'll be exposed to large slices of it within these pages.

If not, be sure to wash your hands before and after thumbing onward.

Do You Have A Brain?

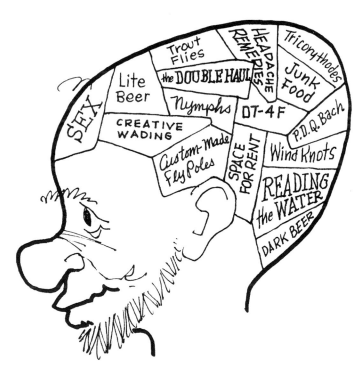

Some fortunate people possess a natural inclination (approximately 15 degrees from vertical) toward fly fishing, while others find it necessary to apply "brain power," or thinking in the headbone, to fully appreciate the sport. In order to best exercise the average angler's cranial capacity it is important to have the various seg-

ments, or lobes, labeled by function, as in the accompanying diagram, so as to avoid confusion. This will assure the efficacious application of the resources pertinent to fly fishing, while the irrelevant sections can safely be left to their own devices, so long as they do not contribute to needless flatulence, wind knots or leaking chest waders.

The brain was invented 1.5 to 3 million years ago in order to expedite mankind's evolution, i.e., the discovery of fire, the pop-top beer can, philosophy, Dolly Parton, and the Swiss Army knife. Despite the passage of considerable time, but a tiny fraction of the brain's awesome capacity is being utilized today, being mostly devoted to sex, lite beer, TV game shows, weight-loss diets, and custom-crafted bamboo fly rods.

Incidentally, the left lobe of the brain controls the right, or casting hand (unless you are left-handed). Not many fishers are aware of this. Even fewer care.

Piscatorial Pachyderms

Fly fishing is akin to painting an elephant; there always seems just a bit more of the subject to cover. This may account for the fact that you see so few elephants on fishing streams today. Then, again, it may not.

It is a pity that pachyderms are not more fully utilized by fly fishers, for they are truly the original off-road vehicle, being responsible for Hannibal's trans-Alpine sortie of 247 B.C., when he contrived to transport his fly-casting team to the Rome Games. They proved excellent at crossing streams, conquering rough terrain and, even in the face of poor roads, got good mileage out of limited hay. Probably their later lag in popularity stemmed from their lack of an effective emission-control system.

If you are looking for a capable recreational vehicle, the elephant should be given consideration as an alternative to the ubiquitous 4-wheel-drive vehicles cluttering the back country today.

The illustration shows Louisa, current staff elephant, guide, and fish retriever for The River's Edge, a fly-fishing shop in Bozeman, Montana, where Greg Lilly claims she is one of his more dependable employees, never losing a client or missing a meal. A few selected Ford dealerships are franchised to handle elephants, as are some U-drive agencies in larger cities in the Northwest. Both new and used pachyderm sales have been lethargic this year, accounting, in part, for our trade imbalance with some third-world elephant-exporting nations.

A "buy American" attitude, however, should not deter you from considering an elephant for your own garage. Remember, they are environmentally compatible and, when used up, biodegradable.

Nearly everyone leaping into the fly-fishing game, after purchasing a rod, line, one leader and three flies, expects instantly to be capable of casting 126 feet or more. This is somewhat difficult until you spend at least 12 minutes perfecting:

The Highly Regarded Double-Haul Cast

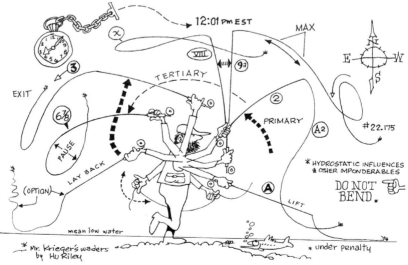

Accomplishing the famed "double haul" is very much like your first sexual encounter: all the best of intentions and high expectations, but mostly ending up all elbows and knuckles and heavy breathing. Some people are better at it than others,

the double haul, I mean. When done right it's quite rewarding, and gives you a sense of power and accomplishment.

A few casters catch on quickly; others labor long and frustratingly before getting the hang of it. Many never make it, being physically or mentally unable to grasp the complex dynamics of the act. If you can pat your skull with one hand, while rubbing your stomach with the other, as Mel Krieger, master teacher of the double haul, points out, you may just have the combined aptness necessary for success.

Don't become intimidated, however, for with proper breathing and loose, comfortable clothing, you will find the double haul only hazardous to the health of bystanders or passing mooses, or meese. Keep in mind, as well, that many fine fishermen I have known, such as Milford Poltroon, failed utterly to master the double haul, but were more or less successful at other pursuits, like peddling peanut butter, picking non-lethal mushrooms and creative resting.

Milford could sit on a grassy stream bank, completely inert, observing the *Baetis* or moose hatches, and quaffing beer better than any other angler in my memory, all without so much as a passing thought for the double haul.

In the accompanying diagram, Mel Krieger, foremost exponent of the double haul as a touchstone to a rich and happy life, delineates the various movements necessary in making a viable and effective cast, using only a conventional greenheart fishing pole, Velcro fasteners and a portable microwave oven. Mel claims this is no more difficult than it looks. Krieger has taught this technique to such luminaries as Ed Zern, Steve Rajeff, the entire Gabor family, and Jimmy Carter, who wrote feelingly:

Dear Mel:

The thrill of having been President of the U. of S.A. is mere peanuts compared to the power and prestige I now feel, having, thanks to you, mastered the double haul.

Keep the faith,
Jimmy

The Great Fly Fishing Fraud

You probably got conned into this fly-fishing game by grace of viewing a TV piscator catching awesome numbers of bass, tarpoons and trout fishes using only a fly pole and cameraman. Or you may have read the highly exaggerated adventures of fly fishers afield and astream in periodicals like *Afield and Astream*, The *Fly Dangler* and *Haberdashers Weekly.* If you believe that you, too, can enjoy and duplicate these artful exploits just by purchasing a fly rod and sallying forth, you are going to be, alas, disappointed, yes.

First (1st), you must recognize that these storytellers are, for the most part, professionals. By that I mean fishing pros or writing pros (although occasionally they are pro orthodontists, proctologists or barristers who fish first, write second, and ortho, procto, or litigate merely to support their fishing habits), and can be relied upon to overwhelm you with the romance (and availability) of their adventures.

In the second (2th) inst., were you to try retracing their boot tracks, you most likely would find the fabulous fishspots they extol pretty much fished out, or posted against trespass, or at least 4,000 miles (and $4,000) away.

Thirdly, nearly all thrilling fishaction pictures are phony frauds or set-ups in which a large, frozen fish is brought along to the appropriately photogenic site, and artfully articulated between the angler and the camera, with plenty of watery droplets and, in the case of video recording, heart-stimulating sound.

Last, a good many of the great fishing waters described in glowing phrases and graphics do not actually exist, but rather are figmentations of some outdoor writer's inventive headbone, plus the collusion of certain unscrupulous photographers, who will risk reputation for an ill-gotten buck or choice steelhead filet.

Thus, as an eager beginner, you must accept the reality that you will, over considerable time, exercise your budding skill enthusiastically casting over essentially fish-free waters.

Unless, of course, you are a proctologist.

An Entire Chapter Devoted to Getting Lost

One of Yellowstone Park's beloved Meese, Fred, claims never to have been "lost" since the installation of the Natl. Park's thoughtful Sustained Yield Loss program in '81, making the forest virtually loss-proof.

Getting lost in the woods is remarkably easy. However, most people who do so become needlessly panicked, thrashing about aimlessly, looking for North, telephone booths, sidewalks with wheelchair ramps, and other signs of civilization. What they should be doing is applying basic woods lore, moving purposefully, and observing the animals.

Animals rarely get lost. I have yet to hear of a "lost" elk, puma or pocket gopher. Animals tend to be deliberate, just plodding along in whatever direction they were headed, until they encounter a freeway and follow it home, or at least to the first gas station, where they can ask directions. Humans (i.e., fly fishers), not blessed with this animal "instinct," would be well advised to learn basic methods for ascertaining where they are.

Among items of woods lore you should know are the facts that:

- Streams generally flow downhill, unless otherwise posted; lakes and other bodies of water do not.
- There are more than 34 million traffic signals in this country; you're never far from one.
- Navigating by the stars is difficult in the woods, due to trees; the Forest Service is attempting to rectify this.
- Edible roots and berries are ever available for sustenance; watch what the bison and gophers eat.
- Watch for marks on trees, i.e., No Trespassing signs, others saying "Bozeman, 13 mi.," "Mom's Cafe," and "Luke loves Irma," all denoting nearness to cultural centers.

Should you plan to get lost, be sure you are properly equipped with the following items of survival equipment:

2 lbs. dried pinto beans	8-foot stepladder
Chainsaw and file	Map of downtown Las Vegas
50 feet binder twine	1 liter lighter fluid
Coffee pot	Can of tomato sauce
Bugle or harmonica	Wok
1 doz. sesame hot dog buns	3 lbs. peanut brittle
Pitching horseshoes	Credit cards

For getting properly lost, maps are indispensable, as they give you a feeling of confidence. Maps tend to identify graphically the various physical features you will likely encounter on the ground. Clearly depicted are such recognizable items as freeways, villages, mountain ranges, bodies of water, abandoned railway whistle-stops, nuclear testing sites, national parks and points of historical significance. A handy reference index usually is printed over the segment of the map you were most interested in looking at. Locating yourself on the map (you are here-X) can be a most rewarding experience.

Maps go all the way back to Egypt and Ptolemy, who did a quite creditable job of cartography on the world of that day, so long as one did not stray too far from Alexandria. However, a goodly number of fishermen got lost following Ptolemy's directions. The map shown here, thought to be the work of Ptolemy, depicts the known

world of that time (A.D. 150), when it was generally agreed that West Yellowstone, Montana, wherever that is, was the center of the universe, and that the sun and satellites orbited around it. Recently scholars have determined that the center has shifted approximately 81.5 kilometers south, to the vicinity of Felt, Ida., closer to the fine fly fishing on the Henry's Fork.

Were he around today, Ptolemy would be pleased to note that modern scientific investigation has proved the world to be indeed flat, made of asphalt and, if one ventures beyond Winnemucca, one will fall off the edge.

Later maps were much more sophisticated, made on Mercator's projection, a cunning method of limning the known world on the skin of an orange, then peeling it off to lie flat. Mercator's maps had the habit of showing Iceland as being approximately 42 times the size of Texas, which was largely responsible for starting the Spanish-American war.

Today's outdoorsmen can rely on more detailed and accurate maps, without all those little gods blowing winds, and often confusing Latin terms, like Tropicus Capricorni, Philadelphia or Pocatello.

Exceptionally good for getting lost by are U.S. Geological Survey topographic maps, which show land contours with little brown lines, water in blue, and defunct mining towns. Many of these were published in 1895, reprinted in 1940, and lack freeways, an altogether more pleasing landscape than the one we know now.

Footnotes

You will note that the margins of many of the following pages are cluttered up with "footnotes" (see *) which purport to reinforce or elaborate upon the noticeably weak

text. I've always enjoyed footnotes and once passed a history course (with an abominably dull textbook) merely by absorbing the footnotes.

Glancing at footnotes, usually in small type, also affords excellent eye exercise, which may later measurably improve your ability to see, at one and the same time, your size 18 Adams being inhaled by a largish rainbow, as well as your boot-clad foot sliding off the moss-slick boulder on which you were standing.

Plenty of informative information lurks in these footnotes, so PLEASE PAY ATTENTION.

A SAMPLE FOOTNOTE: Never attempt to put peanut butter on a pickle; it just slides off. However, a pickle, embedded in peanut butter on a slice of salt-rising bread, is a gourmand's delight.

Lefty

Hardly a week goes by when I am not stopped in a Safeway parking lot, or while jay walking across a busy thoroughfare to a nearby saloon, by some stranger asking: "Aren't you Bernard "Lefty" Kreh and will you teach me to fly cast in three minutes?" Despite the fact that Lefty is only 168 centimeters tall and has never shot a wild turkey, there is little resemblance between us, and I rarely chide a stranger for this mistaken identity, but rather do as Lefty would do under the circumstances: TEACH.

Since every recruit to fly fishing means one less involved in hubcap-theft gangs, wine-tasting parties and political-action groups, I am ever willing to spend as much as seven minutes of my valuable fishing or salooning time teaching strangers all I know about fly casting, entomology, stream reading, ecosystem management, wind knots, etc., confident that I am contributing to a better, more cultured world. Lefty feels the same way, except on Tuesdays, his fishing days.*

Fly casting, the admired art and fundamental challenge of our sport, can be learned as easily as de-horning cattle. It is no more difficult than becoming a taxidermist or editorial cartoonist, or raising live seahorses for fun and profit.

The basic act of casting could be described as a rhythmic fore-and-aft movement of the forearm and wrist so that the rod is flexed in such manner as to propel the line and fly back and also forth until they arrive ultimately in the vicinity of the target fish. Then again, it can be called flailing. But flailing with finesse.

Lefty Kreh's well-known cap shades not only his eyeballs, but a six-square-foot area to the north from harmful semi-violet rays, which can ricochet off his highly reflective nose, irritating and repulsing fish and other things.

Kreh's patented casting grip, hazardous
in the hands of amateurs, can be used
only with his written permission.

The act of casting is relatively simple, until you complicate it by introducing the several laws of physics pertinent thereto:

- **NEWTON'S LAW OF MOTION:** A fly rod, dropped from an apple tree, will fall at twice the speed of sound, always landing point-first and breaking off four inches of the tip.
- **FOLGER'S LAW OF HYDRODYNAMICS:** Chest waders will leak only when immersed in water.
- **McLAUGHLIN'S LAW OF DIMINISHING RETURNS:** Always buy or tie three flies of any one pattern—one for the ear, one for the brush behind you, and one for the fish.
- Also be mindful of **POLTROON'S LAW** (available in poster size, unsuitable for framing, $29.95 ppd. Order now, supply limited): "He who false casts deceives only himself."

Some liken the arm motion, called the "casting stroke," to:

Swatting flies	Hurling the javelin
Cranking a Model T	Chopping firewood
Beating wives	Waving good-bye

In the unlikely event that you could combine all the above into a single set of movements of the wrist, thumb, triceps, latissimus dorsii, and gluteus maximus, you might come up with an appropriate casting stroke. Then again, probably not, for the act of making the fly rod do its thing properly is unique, and calls upon a controlled use of muscles you never knew you owned.

Rarely photographed because of his unconquerable fear of the evil spirits lurking in cameras, Lefty Kreh here shyly demonstrates the Hasselblad Parallelogram cast, in which the DT-12 fluorescent fuchsia line is persuaded to remain suspended in the air in order to be clearly captured on Panatomic-X film by well-known wildlife photographer David Eisendrath, utilizing an Argus C-3 with 1000mm telephoto lens and dedicated flash at F-8 at a 50th sec.

You will find that a rudimentary knowledge of hydrodynamics, aerobics, Kung Fu and pedomancy can come in handy, as well as maintaining a nutritious diet, with much fiber and lecithin, to ensure the necessary energy. A belief in God and a rewarding after-life may be of help. Drinking lite beer, according to three respected doctor/anglers, has little, if any, effect. Wearing comfortable clothing, breathing deeply, and keeping clean thoughts is known to be efficacious. And carry a valid credit card.

*FOOTNOTE: Bernard "Lefty" Kreh actually is right-handed, but, to preserve his image, wears specially tailored T-shirts on which quaint sayings such as "I'd rather be bonefishing" and "Angleworms are man's best friends" are printed backwards, so that photos of Lefty can be reversed to show him casting left-handed. Familiarity with little-known facts such as this is what makes fly fishing the glamorous sport it is thought to be.

More about Casting

As in any other sport, the terminology of fly fishing is a good part of the game. For instance, learning the names of the various "casts" often can make you the center of attention at cocktail parties or political conventions. Take, for example, the well-known "roll cast," the first thing you must learn before becoming an accomplished caster.

The roll cast was inadvertently invented by Sir Cedric Parker-House in 1766, whilst fishing for brown trout on the Itchen*. During a period of spate and stiff breezes, he noted trout rising vigorously to crumpets, blown into the stream from a buffet luncheon on the nearby fen. Sir Cedric found that by cunningly impaling a bor-

This early prototype of **WULFF'S PATENTED BACKCAST ENFORCER** here is operated by the late Lee Wulff and his faithful accomplice, Joan, to show how to control the maximum extent a backcast is allowed to drift rearward before "cracking the whip" and beginning the forecast. Much improved recent models with microchips, quartz movements and a sun roof are available at most advanced tackle shops and through mail-order catalogs. Batteries not included.

21

rowed crumpet on his size 13 Cock Y' Bondhu, he was able to entice, hook, and land several respectable browns to seven kilos. When asked to identify his lure, Sir Cedric replied: "Nailed the buggers on a cast roll, by Gad, sir." Thus came to fame the "Parker-House Roll." Recent independent studies have shown that Twinkies and corn dogs are equally effective.

*ANOTHER FOOTNOTE: Very few people know how the River Itchen got its name. I certainly don't. The Mississippi and the Great Gray Greasy Limpopo fall into the same category. Neither are particularly good fly-fishing streams.

The Esthetic Appeal of Fly Casting

Almost everyone who ventures into the fly-fishing game does so because of the obvious esthetic image created by the competent fly caster at work. Ah, the fluidity, the grace and rhythm of the fly rod, the smooth looping of the line, the flawless turnover of the fly, and its easy descent upon the water. I can do that, you say, and so commit to the sport, presuming you will, in but a few easy lessons, or books read, or weekends spent, become, voila, a fly fisher. Ha!

Unlike painting, writing poetry or inventing the steam calliope, very few people are born fly casters. Even the swiftest learners take more than a couple weeks' practice before they become a Lefty Kreh or Steve Rajeff, or even an Al Poltroon (who holds the world record for false casts in a West Yellowstone phone booth). Before becoming the superb caster you wish to be, you will have to undergo the agonies of mastering simple, basic—if seemingly stupid—actions and maneuvers of wrist, rod, and line, all of which are preludes to accomplishing those fluid and even ballet-like motions associated with the mature fly cast.

Some people never make it, being physically or temperamentally unsuited to any athletic effort beyond stamp collecting, quoits or

hang gliding. Others, who persevere in learning the rudiments and spend considerable time in practice, may arrive at that rewarding moment when they can pick up a fly rod, flex it properly, point it in the general direction of a body of water, and have the attached fly arc in grace and beauty to the appointed place, somewhere near a rising fish's open mouth. According to how diligent one is, this moment may occur anywhere from the second week of apprenticeship up to or beyond the dozenth year of application.

A Fly Fisher's Ten Commandments

I. Thou shalt not adulterate thy fly with bits of rotating metal, nor juice of egg, nor segment of worm.

II. Thou shalt not covet thy neighbor's superbly crafted bamboo rod, his leak-free waders, or his well-built, fly-tying wife.

III. Thou shalt not cadge a fellow angler's successful and better-tied flies, without reciprocating with at least a six-pack.

IV. Thou shalt not muscle in on another angler's water, except where trout are rising openly to his fly.

V. Thou shalt not lie to a fellow fisher when asked, "What fly pattern are they taking?" without smiling.

VI. Thou shalt not filch from a six-pack cached in the stream, unless it can be ascertained to belong to a worm fisherman.

VII. Thou shalt not snag with your fly passing boatmen, water skiers, inner tubers or small, rock-throwing urchins, except by chance.*

VIII. Thou shalt not shut the car door or trunk lid on a companion's favorite fly rod, unless simultaneously doing so to your own.

IX. Thou shalt not curse thy gear for thy foul luck; thy rod casteth where thou pointeth, thy leader breaketh at thy badly tied knot, and thy boot slippeth because thou faileth to plant it with appropriate caution on the slippery @#$%&! rock.

X. Thou shalt not forsake thy responsibility to family and community to slake thy thirst for fishing without ample reason (and there are at least 67 cunningly hidden in the following pages).

*YET ANOTHER FOOTNOTE: The odds for snagging an invading boatman are not bad for the average caster. Small children take much more practice.

Waders

I know of but few fishers, no matter how accomplished, who can walk on water easily. Most of us must cope with water, a necessary component of most streams and ponds, by the use of hip boots or chest waders, unless we elect to fish wet and get chilled and end the day with prune-like calves.

Hip boots have their shortcomings, at around three feet. Chest-high waders, on the other hand, can get you into deep water, often deeper than planned. They are also splendid for retaining perspiration.

Sometimes waders come from the factory already leaking, but most can be relied upon to repel water until immersed for the first time, or when subjected to such threatening objects as barbed wire, beaver-sharpened twigs, or even irate beavers.

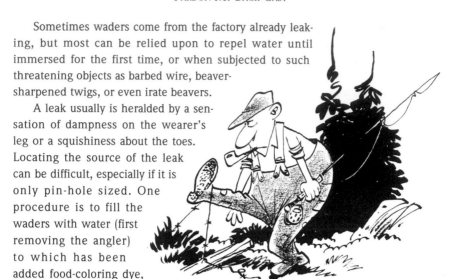

A leak usually is heralded by a sensation of dampness on the wearer's leg or a squishiness about the toes. Locating the source of the leak can be difficult, especially if it is only pin-hole sized. One procedure is to fill the waders with water (first removing the angler) to which has been added food-coloring dye, seltzer, or marshmallow syrup, which will appear either as colorful, bubbly, or sticky evidence at the point of leakage. Most common leaks can be repaired by use of a common leak-repair kit, available at most any reputable leak-repair-kit store.

Temporarily, a leak can be patched using electrician's tape, pitch, goombah or, when available, POOT, (Poltroon's Original Oat Treat, Milford Poltroon's much-loved, stick-to-your-ribs breakfast dish). Some leaks, especially those devilish ones around the crotch seams, will defy repair in spite of your best attentions. Waders that survive beyond a single season prove only that you are not fishing enough.

Today's chest waders are mostly manufactured in foreign lands, and foreign people are used as models to obtain size measurements. Usually these people are inexpensive small children or sumo wrestlers. Thus we are beset with S, M, L & XL sizes all with size-5 feet and crotches in decidedly un-American locations.

Waders do not come equipped with zippers. If you or any of your friends or relatives have a workable solution to this problem, by all means.

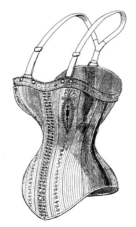

Earliest chest waders developed by the Orvis Tire & Catalog Company were less than successful, due to certain shortcomings. Much improved later models boasted non-skid soles, and proved to be quite popular among the fly-fishing elite.

Creative Wading, Part MXIIV

When the most recent ice sheet finally receded at the tag-end of the Pleistocene era, it left the landscape gouged up pretty much as it is today, except for the freeways and parking lots and attendant evidences of civilization like gas stations and drive-in banks. It also left a legacy of nicely rounded and polished boulders, most of which gravitated to the stream beds, there to lie patiently in wait for passing fishermen, innocent or wary alike.

Varying from buckshot up through Volkswagen size, all these rocks maintain a certain ball-bearing configuration, affording considerable hazard to the health and balance of the wading angler. Even the most confident waders occasionally become de-stabilized by that most insidious of bottom dwellers, the movable rock, some of which are not only capable of writhing impulsively underfoot, but often can achieve surprising bursts of speed in maneuvering around behind you just as you get settled into a comfortable casting stance. A few really agile rocks can actually lash out to grasp passing ankles in a vise-like grip, and fell the unwary.

Rock size, too, can be deceiving. I have had even outhouse-size dornicks, obviously firmly anchored for centuries, tilt flagrantly under my boots, threatening to pitch me into the stream. How they managed to maintain equilibrium on such a delicate pivot point over the years, just waiting for me to come along, I dunno, but I have become skeptical of those that seem most solidly footed.

Except in the most sterile streams, most boulders grow fine coats of nutritious algae or moss, or accumulate a gloss of Vaseline-like silt, all acting as fine wader lubricants. On a number of popular rivers, devoid of this natural slipperiness, the locals are known to go about stealthily at night, applying axle grease to streambed boulders to discourage out-of-town anglers. This practice is illegal in many parts of the country, but the law is largely ignored. Oregon and Washington have a tacit interstate agreement for reciprocal streambed boulder greasing, which has caused much lack of friction for waders in both states.

Whether you wear chest waders, hip boots, or just wading shoes, you should have slick-resistant soles for comfortable and confident wading. Rubber and rocks do not go together well at all. Felt soles or outdoor carpeting suffice for traction on most streams, but some rivers call for the extra grip of metal studs, calks or cleats. But none of these are totally skidproof, and should not inspire the overconfident to go charging astream willy nilly. The judicious, the cautious, the chicken wader will have a longer, more comfortable, undunked angling life. Wade gingerly, and suspect every rock.

Streambed of the Deschutes River, Oregon, looking Southeast.

Creative Wading, Part CLXVI

Despite all caution, one occasionally gets dunked. Whether flirting with fate by wading deceptively deep and swift waters, or just coming a cropper on a nicely Vaselined rock, I have sometimes become upended, and found myself at the mercy of the river.

Now many fishers, when inundated, become anxious, even panicky, and begin to thrash about, gulp in quantities of water, and otherwise make semi-fatal gestures. Not I. After many an unseemly submergence, I have assumed a rather casual attitude toward the inevitable swim. Fortunately, I am blessed with an excellent body-fat content, and tend to float well. Also I can if necessary rely on a strong modified backstroke, and I always wear a wader belt, unless encased in my snug Neoprenes, which don't allow much intruding water to dilute the sweat.

On one memorable occasion I comported myself with considerable dignity on the lower Madison River, the renowned Montana blue-ribbon dunking water, while at the same time providing entertainment for witnesses on the bank. I had waded the Eight-Mile Ford, above Ennis, and spent several enjoyable hours fishing the "splits" upstream. The rainbows and browns had been cooperative, despite a warm and consistent drizzle, and I was sweaty and leg-weary when I returned to the ford. The crossing there is not marked with appropriate pedestrian-crossing white lines, but retracing

my earlier route seemingly posed no great problem. I waded confidently into the swift, navel-deep current. Suddenly one of the river's famed movable rocks attacked, unplanting my upstream foot, causing the other boot to release its grip on the bottom.

There went I, awkwardly bouncing downstream in an embarrassing non-upright position. Though the water was only six feet deep or so, it was difficult to maintain any contact with the riverbed, and the tippy-toe method was pretty much out. So I assumed the relaxed, quasi-tuck position on approaching the bluff downstream, where I noticed a small audience gathered to watch my progress. Utilizing my paddling hand, the other clutching the fly rod of course, I tipped my cap to the sound of polite applause, drifted off downriver, then resumed paddling.

Another fifty yards, and my boots finally found bottom often enough for me to maneuver toward shore, and eventually beach my hulk. I had, of course, a very soggy shirt, and vest pockets well filled, but had shipped only a pint in the waders. Thus ended the float with no fatal results except a limp and useless cigar.

You understand that I don't particularly recommend this system as a desirable form of recreation, but when confronted with such circumstances if you remain calm and apply certain flotation principles, plus prayer if you are so inclined, only embarrassment will result.

As one of my Celtic progenitors, McTavish Poltroon, once said, "If you dinna float good, wade only the wee waters."

General Procedures for Successfully Falling In:

1. Face your unplanned upending with calm and confidence. Think optimistically.

2. Do not give serious consideration to your gear; any reputable tackle shop will be happy to resupply you. Attempting to save your gear at the expense of yourself

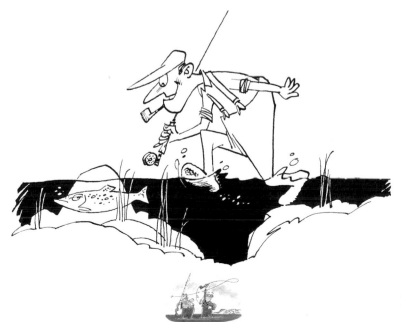

may force you to resort to the services of a medical rescue team, an experience that can be not only harrowing but considerably more costly.

3. Do not succumb to needless panicky flailing. Relax, assume a comfortable position, breathe easily as needed.

4. Do not contest the current. Float in a slight tuck—remember, your buoyant fat content is generally concentrated in your middle and butt sections and tends to pop to the surface, while your head, unless you are notably fat-headed, will sink undesirably. Your feet should be in position to fend off any boulders or other in-stream hazards. Upon arriving in shallower water you may lower your feet in order to locate bottom, at which point you may assume a more upright position, and recapture your dignity as you flounder to the beach or bank.

5. Then, and only then, you may assess the amount of water shipped or ingested, and check what gear is missing. You may also take several deep breaths so as to bring your pulse rate back to normal. This also is the moment when you may wish to imbibe a bit of strong spirits to fight off possible hypothermia and celebrate a successful float.

A Word about Adhesives

There are times when I feel that the world is glued together. I mean, we're surrounded by stuff stuck to other stuff by adhesives of one kind or another, temporarily or permanently. This is probably to the good, as there are many things that can't readily be nailed down, riveted, or wrapped with baling wire.

It likely all started with pitch. I know early man stuck his boats together and waterproofed them with it. Then there was tar, which also had marine applications, as well as fixing yurt seams. Later, paste was developed, for pasting things, and terrible-tasting mucilage, for adhering postage stamps to letters after both were invented. What medieval fishermen used to affix indoor-outdoor carpeting to their boots is not known, but it probably was no more effective than today's adhesives.

Today's high technology has produced some phenomenal products for holding things up or together. Some claim to be capable of gluing an elephant to the ceiling, anchoring tiles on the noses of spacecraft, and holding foreign-made parts to American-made autos. I'm skeptical of all of these, given our lack of success in the matter of persuading carpeting to stay put on wading shoes.

Not only do we still have bad-tasting adhesive to lick and stick on postage stamps, which fall off if you don't want them to, or cannot be pried off in uncancelled form for re-use, we also have super glues to stick your fingers together. There are also waterproof glues that are fine, so long as you don't go near water. Then there are those self-adhering little pot holder hooks to hang on your refrigerator, and the ubiquitous bumper stickers, which either won't stick or cannot possibly be removed except along with the finish. Finally, there are the tapes, Scotch (R), masking, and duct. These, we could hardly do without, but they have their limitations—except for that marvelously sticky price tape put on retail items in your favorite hardware store, which absolutely defies removal.

It is possible, I must assume, that our advancing society will produce new and more powerful adhesives, capable of sticking the things together that we really wish to stick together. I look forward to the day when we can confidently stick:

Toupees to bald skulls	Garden-hose repair sections
Auto mufflers to rusted-out tailpipes	Framed pictures to painted walls
Gloves to small boys	Paper plates to picnic tables
Caps on glue tubes	Guides on fly rods
Patches on wader crotches	

Maybe we can even hope for postage stamps that affix themselves firmly, automatically, without aid of a human tongue, yet slip off effortlessly when uncancelled so they are again usable.

This optimistic outlook may well be unwarranted. More likely we will be stuck with old, tried, and found-wanting adhesives like chewing gum, the residue in the bottom of a coffee cup, barbecue grill goo, strawberry jam, shoe-sole dog doo, aged rubber bands, and candy bars left in the glove compartment.

How to Find West Yellowstone

Some of the splendidest trout fishing in the country (as contrasted to urban trout fishing) is to be found near West Yellowstone, Montana, wherever that is*. Locating W. Yel. on most maps and gazeteers is not all that difficult, yet getting there by any means can be arduous, if not impossible, which accounts for the good fishing.

Commercial aircraft are known to arrive sporadically at the famed W. Yellowstone Bearport, sometimes carrying passengers, but more often bearing only luggage destined for Great Falls, Denver, or Auckland. Planes actually landing are warned against unprovoked attacks by itinerant moose (meese?). Occasionally planes headed for Great Falls or Butte will waggle their wings at the natives as they pass over.

Since the rails were sold to Japan for scrap before World War II, there has been no passenger train service to West Yel., and the former richly appointed depot was converted into a fly-fishing museum and snowmobile warehouse. So traveling by rail is not advised.

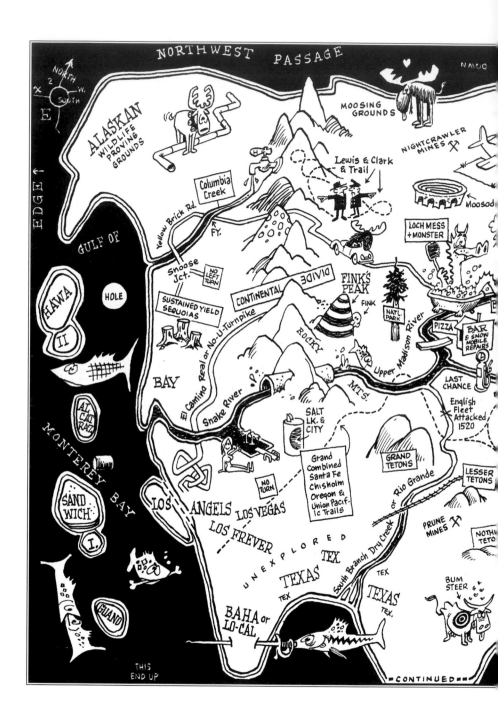

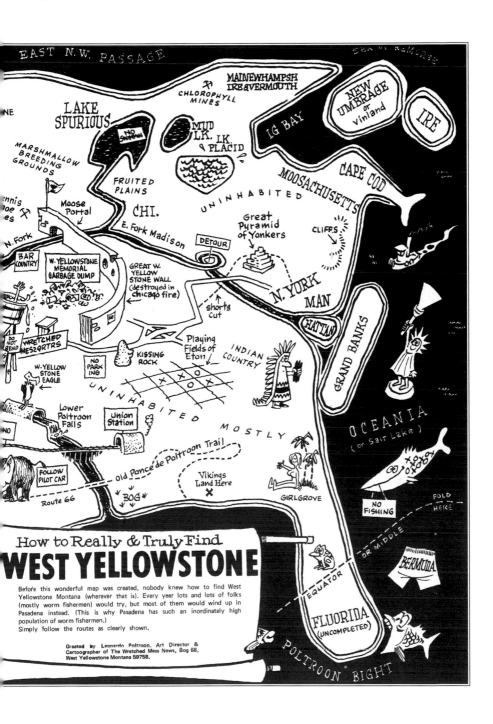

How to Really & Truly Find
WEST YELLOWSTONE

Before this wonderful map was created, nobody knew how to find West Yellowstone Montana (wherever that is). Every year lots and lots of folks (mostly worm fishermen) would try, but most of them would wind up in Pasadena instead. (This is why Pasadena has such an inordinately high population of worm fishermen.)
Simply follow the routes as clearly shown.

Created by Leonardo Poltroon, Art Director & Cartographer of The Wretched Mess News, Bog 68, West Yellowstone Montana 59758.

Interstate highways and other roads always seem to go elsewhere, so reaching W. Yellowstone by auto, bus, pickup, or motor home is quite out of reason. Thus it is hard to explain just how all the millions of vehicles find their way there each summer, to clutter up Yellowstone Natl. Park, irritate the native bison and indigenous W. Yellowstognians, and clog the local fishing waters with their rancid bodies and cast-off plastic wraps. If you must drive, it is suggested that you try Arizona or Ohio, much easier to reach by road.

When steam boating ceased to be economic on the Missouri, West Yel's access to the sea was severely cut off. Therefore, it is no longer practicable to approach the area by water, except by judicious use of a float tube, which requires rather extensive portages.

Bikers, of the pedal persuasion, have been known to make it to W. Yel., but no one has actually seen them en route, except once when two young, buxom cyclists were observed in Fargo, N.D., asking directions, to St. Louis. Fishing from a moving bicycle, however, is prohibited in West Yellowstone and its tributaries.

Other methods not recommended for getting to W. Yello. are by:

Hang glider	Cruise ship
Llama	Skateboard**
Ox team	

*STILL ANOTHER FOOTNOTE: "Montana, wherever that is," is a phrase cunningly copyrighted by that famed former piscatorial periodical, *The Wretched Mess News*, to prevent confusion between MT and MA, MD, MI, MN, MS, or even AK.

**AND YET ONE MORE: It is virtually impossible to operate a skateboard while wearing chest waders and carrying a fly rod.

Fishbooks

Back a number of decades, when I was first cutting my teeth on the game of fly fishing, there were only a few dozen books on the subject of which I was aware. My fly-fishing grandfather occasionally would quote from LaBranche or Taverner or the like, to reinforce an opinion of his own. Most of the information on the sport I gleaned from the few magazines of the day like *Outdoor Field & Stream Life*, and from the several popular tackle catalogs extant. None of these sources claimed that becoming a fly fisher was difficult. They intimated that anyone able to read the larger type on a cereal box, lace his own shoes, and stand clear of tall trees when lightning struck could make it as a fly fisherman with ease.

This is still going on, with a proliferation of fishing magazines, along with perhaps 46,318 books (including this one) dealing with one or another aspect of the sport. And fly-fishing schools, as well, have contributed their theme, that a three-day course can result in molding a full-blown fly fisher out of the rawest clay of a Texas oil mogul or Mini-Mart cashier. All this will bring forth an ever-increasing horde of

half-anglers, descending, mosquito-like, on all our fishable waters, thrashing about, hooking each other on the backcast, and altogether disrupting the outdoor scene. There is nothing "easy" about this transition from urban slug to sophisticated out-doorsperson, and don't let anyone tell you otherwise.

Let this book, then, be among the first to let on that (steel yourself) FLY FISHING IS HARD AND, LIKE HOG-DRESSING, GOOD SEX, OR EATING SUSHI, SELDOM DONE WELL THE FIRST TIME.

Great Fish reading

The late, great philosopher, Aristotle, wrote nothing for posterity about fly fish-ing, which is rather disappointing, as he wrote on any and all subjects of the day (*circa* 300 B.C.), and likely would have had something enlightening and philosophi-cal to pass on. For all we know, the trout fishing in Macedonia might have been ter-rific, but went cunningly under publicized, so that Alexander the Great could have great angling all to himself (how do you think he got that name, anyway?). Centuries later, the Romans, it is said, got to throwing hooks, concealed in goose feathers, to fishes rising in certain streams in the North of Italy, but also failed to write of their successes or lack thereof. This autocratic attitude may have contributed to the gener-al decline of morals, fishing, and the Roman Empire.

The first serious outdoor sports writing of record was done by a 15th century nun, Juliana ("Hot Habit") Berners, who did a nice side bar on the angle, fysshyng wythe, in *The Boke of St. Albans*, (Sopwell Publishers, 1456), which never hit the book-of-the-month list.

There still is considerable controversy over Dame Juliana's part in chronicling early day fly fishing, whether she actually cast a fly, or knew one angle from another. Later by some 200 years another Briton, Izaak Walton, wrote his *Compleat Angler*, still revered as the "bible" on fishing, although Charles Cotton did the segment on fly fishing, the first definitive work on the subject and possibly the root cause of most of our modern-day troubles.

Walton triggered a proliferation of fishbooks that since has swamped us with more than 716,374 titles, both in hard and soft cover, dealing with fishy subjects, some 22.5% concerned with fly fishing. This represents one copy for each genus of mayfly, plus enough left over to supply the entire literate population of Bozeman, Montana, the only city in North America where trout can openly and legally be wor-shipped.

I would expect that many more books will be written to satisfy the public's appetite for fly-fishing literature but, of the splendidly long list at hand, I recommend these vital works:

For History:
The Compleat Angler (Walton)
The Dry Fly and Fast Water (LaBranche)
A History of Fly Fishing for Trout (Hills)
The Fishing in Print (Gingrich)

For Flavorful Information:
Quill Gordon (McDonald)
A Trout and Salmon Fisherman for 75 Years (Hewitt)

For Literary Enjoyment:
Any book by Roderick Haig-Brown
The Year of the Angler (Raymond)
Trout Magic (Traver)

For Fun:
A Fine Kettle of Fish Stories (Zern)
How to Fish Good (Poltroon)

A Gold Mine

While performing a routine liver transplant in West Yellowstone's famed Polyclinic and Yamaha Repair Depot on Miss Myrtle Sue Goff, of Felt, Ida., well-known podiatric surgeon Dr. Roy Nakamura struck gold near her pancreas. Elated over the fortunate find, the good doctor staked several claims near the spleen, and found that by installing a small, unobtrusive placer system, the "Myrtle Sue," as they named the mine, could be made to produce up to $27 per day in fine gold.

Dr. Roy and Myrtle Sue were later married in a lavish ceremony in the Reformed Latter Day Born Again Christian Cathedral in Rexburg, after which they built a richly appointed A-frame near Last Chance, where they raised twin daughters, Goldie and Gilda. Now retired, in their "golden years," Dr. Roy and Myrtle Sue operate a part-time spay-and-neuter clinic in Bozeman, Mont., when not guiding wealthy fly fishermen on the nearby Gallatin and Yellowstone rivers.

Identifying Trout Made Easy

Identifying the many and varied species of fishes found in our waters is not overly difficult, except for trout, which mostly look alike. Just as fishermen affect beards and funny clothes, trout have FEATURES. Watch for them.

Some trout are Salmonids. Others are not, but this seems not to bother them. Should you catch a fish with large pointy antlers or heavy fur, rest assured that it is NOT A SALMONID, and should be released forthwith.

Rainbow trout *(Salmo prettypants)* are quickly recognized by their silvery, multi-colored sides. These are not to be confused with silver trout (not a *Salmo*, but an *Oncorhynchus nerka*, or sockeye salmon), which are also silvery, but blush badly when spawning.

Then there are the cutthroats, another kettle of fish entirely, which can be spotted by their numerous spots, or zits, and a trace of lipstick on the chin. The romantic and much-publicized "brookie," or brook trout, is not a trout at all, but rather an invention of several prominent outdoor writers from Michigan or New Hampshire. Brown trout (*Salmo the Hun,* or mean old bastids), are imports from Europe and are often blamed for our present trade deficit, along with Volkswagens and hand-knit ski sweaters. Browns are renowned among fly fishers for their pugnasty nature, and their reverence (like fishers') for nymphs. They also pose nicely for photographs. Steelhead and rainbow trout are considered by biologists to be one and the same, much to the disgust of steelheads, who claim seniority and other things. They can sometimes be told apart because one has fuzzier eyebrows, I forget which.

Often there are other fishes found in trouty waters, to include: Bass, carp, brim, sculpin, minnies, maxies, panfish, whitefish, blackfish, stutefish and lutefisk.

In many places there are no fishes whatsoever, which can resolve the fish-identification problem to a degree.

Reading the Water

The ability to divine where, in any body of water, fishes are apt to be swimming and feeding, is not exactly an exact science. Nor is it totally a matter of dumb luck, though that often is not an inconsiderable factor. Successful fish locating is called "reading the water," but for those of you who already have difficulty with printed "words," this could be termed "ogling the water." You must visually assess the water, i.e., look at the crick, to determine (1) Are there any fish here? (B) Where? and (Y) Is there any way I can get a fly anywhere near the spot? This requires a certain amount of eyestrain, fish knowledge and vitamin B-12.*

Sometimes (but not often) this act is simple, as when there is a good hatch on the water and trout are rising, swirling, leaping, and slurping up various insectivora, marshmallows or floating detritus of one or another ilk. On other occasions (a majority, I'm afraid) scanning the creek reveals no surface life except, perhaps, a beer can bobbing by, or a small boy lurching along in an inner tube. But no visible fish. Here you must apply reasoning with the headbone, search the water for likely spots concealing a hungry trout awaiting lunch. Think, for example, "where would I lie if Big Macs were on my mind?" Look for hamburger-shaped rocks, or arched streamside branches. Also keep an eye peeled for other fishy or foody places, such as: pockets, buckets, big holes, little holes, slicks, vortices, chutes, channels, riffles, crannies, undercuts, overhangs, baubles, bangles and drive-in windows.

Water-reading techniques are dramatically different on large, static bodies of water, such as lakes, ponds, and bayous, or on heavily brined waters of sounds, seas, and oceans. Here one must rely on the sighting of leaping fish, fish-oriented birds

perhaps feeding on baitfish, or other signs, saying "Public Fishing." Fly fishing and reading salt water should best be left for your more experienced years. Start small, reading little creeks, gradually working your way up through branches and forks, to mainstem rivers. At all times wear Polaroid glasses, breathe evenly, and affect inconspicuous, but comfortable clothing.

How to See Fish

When "reading the water" in search of likely spots where fishes lurk, be aware that your eyeballs are not totally trustworthy. Your line of sight, upon entering the water, becomes distorted and can wander off many degrees to the NW, if not watched carefully. This can cause you to believe you see a 2 1/2-pound rainbow over there behind a rock when, in reality, what you are viewing is a plastic English muffin wrapper trailing seductively off an abandoned bedspring well downstream.

This effect does not apply to brown trout, which always seem to be 14 feet behind you, nor to brook trout, which cannot be seen, only sensed, and never where they ought to be. The particular aberration, sometimes called "Kreh's Syndrome," is compounded if you wear bifocals, and has caused many a bespectacled angler to see more trout than actually exist. Ophthalmologists, being familiar with illusions, seldom are bothered with this affliction, or can afford to ignore it. Trout, on the other hand, are constantly bewildered when viewing fishermen, who seem to be either standing on them, or suspended 30 feet overhead in a frightening halo of light.

Anglers should wear polarized glasses**, drink only lite beer, and squint. Trout are advised to do likewise.

Most bodies of moving water give up their secrets readily, showing in their riffles and eddies and obstructions the most obvious spots where cover and food and thus fishes are likely to concentrate. The angler who addresses his casts to these areas can be confident he has favorable odds of raising a fish or two from them.

But there is always the off chance that some maverick fish has not read the water as well as you, and for some reason or other is disporting in an altogether unseemly spot, which you have ignored or even waded into, willy nilly. This happened to me often enough that I tend now to put many casts over obviously sterile waters, peering over my shoulder to make certain no one is watching my seemingly ignorant (and often futile) ways.

Once down in New Zealand I was fishing a lovely little cow-pasture river (yes, they have cows in New Zealand; at least 30 have been counted). The river was drought low, with bleached gravel on the shore, and there was not a tree anywhere to throw shade on the water. It was an honest 90 degrees and I had sweated a mile upstream in increasingly obnoxious and unnecessary waders.

Directly ahead was a stool-sized boulder poking up out of a foot of flat, obviously fishless water. The sun shown straight down on my perspiring headbone, reminding me it was lunch time. I sat down on the rock, and relaxed over a sandwich and a luke-warm beer, admiring the streamside grasses and reflecting on the impossibility of any sane fish (or for that matter, fisherman) being in the immediate vicinity.

My reverie was jolted in mid-swig by the sight of a large fin breaking the surface not a rod's length away, followed by a swirling boil no larger than a garbage can lid, carving a huge hole in what was no more than six inches of water. "Ten thousand blue pipes," I cried, causing several cows to heave to their feet and flee noisily upstream.

Draining the beer, and crushing the can with a feverish burst of energy, I splashed up river in ankle-deep water, just to satisfy myself that I had merely hallucinated, that there was no trout in that ridiculously uninviting water. After I had taken a dozen steps, a huge brown roared across to the questionable shelter of the far bank with a great surge and rooster-tail wake. "Jeez," I scolded myself, "if you can't catch 'em, kick 'em!"

I neither saw nor spooked another fish the rest of the afternoon, but I stopped on my way back down river, and in the failing light, there, sure enough, was this great trout lying in the same spot, obviously content with his choice. A single, well-placed cast managed to spook him once more.

"To hell with you," I murmured, as I plodded off down the meadow.

But at least I saw him.

*THE FIRST OF MORE FOOTNOTES: Consuming quantities of carrots has not been proven to improve water-reading ability appreciably. However, certain mushrooms have been found to give one visions you wouldn't believe.

**THE SECOND OF MORE FOOTNOTES: The use of polarized glasses enables you to see polar bears, Poles, and other approaching underwater ethnic groups, who might interfere with your fishing. They are not effective on anglers of Scandinavian descent who, seemingly, cannot readily be polarized.

Choosing a Fly Rod

Most fishermen spend a great deal more time and thought picking out a fly rod than they do choosing a wife. This may account for the inordinately high rate of divorce among anglers. It is wise, in either case, not to grasp the first attractive item that comes along, for you may have to live with her (rods are feminine, just like wives) for a considerable time. A choice, by whim of the moment, can lead to untold troubles.

Rushing out and purchasing a fly rod is absolutely the wrong first step in becoming a fly fisher. However, it is more fun than going through the more logical ritual of assessing the quarry sought, its taste in flies, the line necessary to cast them, and then, only then, getting down to the one romantic tool needed, the rod.

Rod buying can be a sport unto itself and, if kept under reasonable restraint, will give you many rewarding hours, when the weather is foul, the rivers in spate, or you are at odds with the wife over your extravagances in recreational equipment and must seek more favorable environs, like the local tackle shop.

Over the years I have accumulated more rods than I can possibly use, yet I find myself often in tackle emporia fondling the latest graphite or custom bamboo with giddy, acquisitive thoughts.

One good way to approach the purchase of a rod is to give it a thorough test, take it fishing, or at least cast it a bit. Most tackle shops boggle at such practice, and frown on anything but an in-shop brandishing of the weapon. You end up knocking over displays or poking the proprietor in the eye, altogether unsatisfactory acts for all parties concerned.

For a scientific test you might anchor the rod to a convenient wall, hang an ounce weight to its tip, and calibrate its curve of deflection with a felt-tip pen. This will impress bystanders, but proves only the rod's ability to bend, and how difficult it is to remove felt-tip pen marks from a wall.

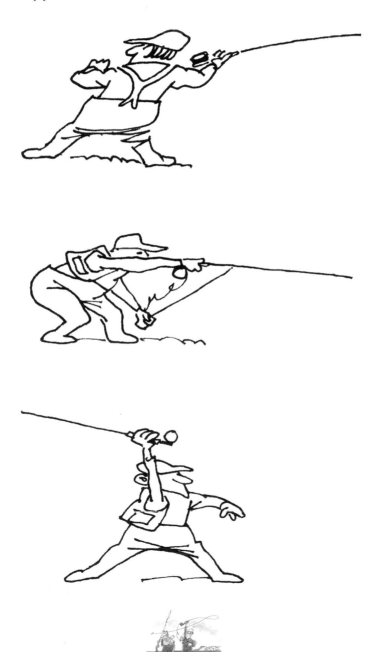

By far the easiest way to acquire a new rod is to have somebody give you one, usually a doting wife or rich relative. Even wives with the best of intentions can succumb to sales, however, and may ignore the specifications you have carefully laid out to come up with something that costs only $29.95 but does not quite fit your desires.

One extremely effective rod-getting method, especially if you shudder at shelling out the bucks demanded for a brand-new graphite, is to borrow. Well-equipped fishing friends can seldom resist when you request the loan of one of their favorite fly rods. Plan to keep the rod for at least a month's testing, and perhaps your friend will forget he loaned it to you. At the moment I have two rods out on loan which, after five years, I never expect to see again. Fortunately, I couldn't cast worth beans with either one, so the loss is not too painful. If the loanees happen to read this, and are still happy and unburdened of conscience, I can only hope their mothers' barking and scratching at the door does not keep them awake at night.

A word of caution: Do not allow yourself to become emotionally involved with a particular rod, for it is an absolute certainty that it will be the one you close the car door on, or spear a streamside log with, or watch fall into the campfire. My long-time fishing companion, Milford Poltroon, was known for always taking along a spare pre-broken rod on each excursion, theorizing that the odds against breaking more than one rod on any given sortie were astronomical. One wonders, though, about the source of his extensive collection of broken fly rods.

Shamans Make Sense

It is known that our indigenous Indian tribes relied heavily on the divinings of their Shamans, or medicine men, to foretell when and where the best hunting and fishing was to be found.

The Shaman would rattle gourds, beat drums, cast bones, or chant fish-and-game-oriented incantations, in order to conjure up a proper vision. "Hiya, hiya, huh, ahuh, ahummahummahum, yuh," they would intone, calling up the gods of bison, prairie chickens, and red salmon. "The buffalo are thick as fleas upon the dog just over the ridge," they would say, or "I see salmon packed as the white man's cord wood over on the South Fork." They would then bless the hunters' arrows or fly rods, and send them afield or astream, as the case might be, confident they would return to camp loaded with protein. Seldom did they miss predicting the right direction to take in order to put game and fish in the lodges.

We latter-day fly fishers sorely lack shamans. Regrettably, we get little help when it comes to choosing a good time and place to go fishing, except for the opinions of tackle-shop proprietors, outdoor writers, and bartenders, none of whom are notably reliable. Even your trusty fishing friends rarely can come up with anything better than "I hear someone got a five-pounder out of Mud Lake last month," or "you shouldda been on the North Fork Wednesday."

Obviously, what we need is a shaman, someone omniscient, trustworthy, and capable of picking the right lake or stream at the right time, like next Wednesday. My own group of troutsters, the Washington Fly Fishing Club, toyed with the idea of

appointing some qualified member as shaman, and we had a great candidate in Andy Gumpertz. An obvious priestly type, he stood a short 260 wader-clad pounds and regarded the world with a fierce visage from blue eyes on either side of a hawk-like beak. He also had a resonant story-telling voice with matching vocabulary. A near-perfect shaman indeed.

Alas, Andy came to an untimely curtain to his long and dramatic angling career, and has removed to that Big Sky country (unfortunately not Montana) where he is likely catching (and releasing) huge browns in that lovely, bountiful trout run hard by the pearly gates. Thus, our club has no other reputable shaman on the immediate horizon.

Unless you have access to a good shaman, remember to:

(A) Trust no one, especially blood relatives.

(2) Do not expect your underarm deodorant to last.

(c) When choosing between two possible fishspots, always flip a two-headed coin.

(9) Keep in mind the famous fish saying of Euripides, god of unpatched waders: "He who casts bread upon the water will certainly catch mostly catfishes."

WE REGRET

this is **NOT** a **LARGE TYPE** edition for those of you with **VISION** problems. If you experience **DIFFICULTY** reading this, we suggest you get a friend or relative to **READ** it to you and **DESCRIBE** the illustrations, so that you may fully **APPRECIATE** the splendid text and graphic material.

E F D T L P

D E F P O T E C

ONCORHYNCHUS

LITE BEER

If you can read these lines you really should consider becoming an airline pilot or microchip inspector, occupations which pay enough to justify the extravagance of being a fly fisher.

Remember that good eyesight is not a necessary requisite for becoming a good fly fisher. Most of us have poor vision and other physical and mental impairments, some of which can be overcome, or at least ignored. The author, some years back, found his eyesight gone to hell; he could no longer see a No. 16 Adams being inhaled at sixty-feet by a five-pound trout. After two interocular implants he can now see a No. 16 Adams at sixty-five feet not being taken by a five-pounder, or, for that matter, a trout of any size.

Food for Fly Fishers

Had I aspired to fame and fortune, I would have made this a diet book. Diet books sell like crazy in contrast to fish books. The best I can do is give you the real skinny on food for fly fishers.

Anglers do eat, but not necessarily wisely. There is a tendency toward junk food, hastily contrived breakfasts, quick lunches, and heavy post-fishing suppers, all dominated by fat, calories, and beer. This is not the balanced nourishment to power an active fisher, no. One does not subsist on peanut-butter sandwiches alone.

Food seldom is a priority item in a fisherman's day, or even in a week spent on lake or stream; tackle, beer, and proper clothing are more important considerations. However, some of my fishing cronies are gourmet chefs as well as being good anglers. They take pride in concocting elegant meals which, through appreciated, take up a good deal of fishing time, both in preparation and consumption, often when the *Baetis* hatch is at its peak. The reverse extreme is the fisher who subsists solely on beer, chips, and Snickers bars, gulped between frenzied casts.

The truth is that a proper diet is very important for fishermen. Without a well-balanced intake of proteins, carbohydrates, vitamins, fiber, and enzymes of one ilk or another, the average angler can easily become imbalanced. When this happens, disaster awaits, especially should the imbalance occur while one is wading fast waters, entering or exiting a canoe, or executing a difficult double-haul cast.

Nutritionally deficient anglers have been known to hook themselves painfully, sprain various ligaments, or rip their waders, merely because of a lack of vitamin B-12 or riboflavin. (Riboflavin has been banned in West Yellowstone since the Great Broccoli Blight of '76, and now is clandestinely imported from Idaho at outrageous black-market prices).

Fiber,* too, is vital. I have witnessed fellow anglers, low on fiber, sprawled helplessly in the brush, or painfully hung up while trying to negotiate a cattle fence. Fiber occurs naturally in green vegetables (but not in West Yellowstone), and in highly advertised breakfast cereals, but beware: Too much fiber can plug you up something awful.

It is not particularly necessary for fishermen to observe the three-squares-a-day ritual, especially should the timing conflict with the "noon rise" or a good hatch. It is quite important, however, to periodically ingest sustenance in order to maintain certain minimum levels of blood sugar, energy, and gas.

A hearty, nutritious breakfast is a must to carry you through the rigors of a day on the stream, fighting swirly currents, wind knots, and mammoth lunkerfishes. A jelly

doughnut, Macmuffin or foot-long hot dog just won't do, no. What you need is a real gut-filling dish like POOT, Poltroon's Original Oat Treat. Here's the recipe:

Into a large (two-gallon) iron pot throw:
Three pounds of old-fashioned oats (not the new quickies).
1 3/4 liters clear mountain water.
Bring the water to a boil, then add:
Six large apples, hacked up into little chunks.
One pound pitted dates, prunes or raisins, chopped.
One huge sweet onion, diced.
Any other loose stuff in the fridge you can't identify.
A little bit of salt and a good bit of cinnamon.

Simmer awhile, then let set and congeal to some degree, but not long enough so's you can't dig it out of the pot easy. Serves 14 hungry anglers, plus two dogs. Any surplus can be used for wader repairs or caulking log cabin chinks.

*FOOTNOTES (CONTINUED): Fiber was invented at an obscure Madison Avenue ad agency back in 1982 by Hiram ("Hi") Fiber, while he was grasping for a novel slogan to apply to his client's products, mainly cardboard breakfast cereals termed "new," "improved" or "ultra-enriched." The prefix "Hi Fiber" caught on quickly and has since been applied lavishly to such diverse products as asphalt roofing, brake lining and fishing poles. Fiber himself has since retired to Taiwan, where he operates the "All Natural Ingredients Fly Shop."

Image of the Fly Fisher

It is widely accepted that fly fishers are elite snobs. This was corroborated by an independent survey of 1,325 households in Felt, Ida. (population 35), during the disastrous 1987 fescue blight. Therefore, when becoming a fly fisher, you must assume some of the affectations recognized as characteristic of the sport. Of particular emphasis are the features which set fly fishers apart from normal (worm-and-bobber anglers, hardware draggers, etc.) fishers: Vestments, tackle, facial expressions, and vocabulary.

Appropriate Dress

Of course one can fish more or less successfully without the aid of any clothing whatsoever, using only a fly rod, and whatever additional gear one can clutch under the armpit. Naked, however, one is subject to windburn, sunburn, excessive dampness, and biting flies. Fish, even phlegmatic brown trout *(Trutta von sepia)*, don't particularly care if an angler is unclad, but they do often fall to giggling or even giving way to gales of laughter, paying no attention to your well-presented fly.

Much as the freedom of nakedness affords, it is nonetheless recommended that proper attire be observed. Some fly fishers tend to dress up for the sport, choosing L.L. Bean whipcords, Eddie Bauer vests, or REI illustrated weather gear. Others dress down, opting for tattered jeans and T-shirts with accent on comfort and to hell with style. A few don't give a damn how they look, but just put on whatever is handy, no matter what the weather or audience. Whichever you choose, it's considered best to start with undergarments—long johns, skivvies, etc.—and work your way out to wool shirts (with long sleeves to combat bugs and brush), sox, rain gear, hats, suspenders, vests, jackets, shoes, boots or whatever.

The wearing of a necktie is not necessary except on very formal angling occasions. Custom-tailoring, however, does set you apart as one with taste, or at least a positive checking-account balance. But the real secret of a good snobbish image rests on "matched apparel." One just does not sport a red plaid shirt with yellow suspenders, green waders, and a blue ball cap with a puce "CAT" emblem—an awful clash of color and pattern. The headgear should always match either shirt or suspenders. Chest waders must be patched only with matching material, and then as unobtrusively as possible. A clean vest is *de rigeur*, to properly show off emblems of the clubs you belong to, and the exotic fishing spots you may or may not have visited. Creased trousers are acceptable for semi-urban display, or in higher-class taverns,

but when you are actually astream or afield, and unlikely to encounter the impressionable, you can go back to comfort and wear tenny runners and cut-off Levis. If you feel up to it, a tall Stetson, properly sweat-stained, points you out as a rugged fly angler, except in Montana, where you could easily be mistaken for a real-estate broker or pizza-delivery person.

Tackle and Gear

Like tusks on a wart hog, and flashing blue lights on a patrol car, the tackle carried by an angler readily identifies him or her as a fly fisher. No other fishermen would be caught in public openly displaying the assorted gonk festooning an average fly flitter's vest: clippers, hemostat, leader dispenser, loupe, DeLiar, folding wading staff, collapsible net, and wine screw. This equipment tends to make the fly fisher as inconspicuous as horse apples in a phone booth.

The new fly fisher may feel compelled to acquire one each of every item in a tackle catalog in order to become a competent angler, on the theory that tackle makes the fisherman. Nonsense. Also very expensive nonsense. In actual true fact, one can be well enough equipped with only a rod, reel, line, leader and 3 flies, at least momentarily. Once hooked, however, one must recognize that purchasing additional tackle is not only necessary, but half the fun of fly fishing.

Say it with a Sneer

As necessary as are the bodily attributes, one must regard facial expressions as equally important in creating the proper fly fisher's image. Strive for a look of disdain and superiority, especially when in company of bait fishers or drinkers of lite beer. An appropriately supercilious glance can be learned, with adequate practice before the mirror while shaving, but some anglers are blessed with a natural ability to sneer. This can be a matter of genetics, attributed in many cases to the fact that your mother possessed an aristocratic eye, or your father sneered well. A good beard can be helpful, for it not only can conceal a recessive chin, but frame a curled lip to advantage, giving one the appearance of professorial sagacity, as well as affording protection from sunburn and biting insects.

Communicating with Words and Phrases

No matter how effective outward appearances and expressions may be in projecting a proper image, they should be augmented with the rich and recognizable vocabulary of fly fishing. This immediately will set you apart from the usual saloon conversationalists, with their glottal grunts and y'knows. You would be surprised how quickly rapport and new friendships can be established in bars, gas stations, and airport baggage carousels, at the dropping of such terms as "Caddis hatch," "Graphite-Boron," and "Schwiebert." Your identity as a master fly fisher is almost assured when you commit to memory the following:

LUNKER: Any fish that broke your leader and got away.
SMOLT: An old smelt.
BELLY: The fat part of a fly line or a fisherman.
CALLIBAETIS: Any unidentifiable bug.
TIP: Unreliable fish information.
TIPPET: Unreliable fish information from a female.
IZAAK WALTON: Uncle of a famous professional basketball player.
LEFTY: An unfortunate chain sawyer.
WULFF: A mythological fly fisherman.
TERRESTRIAL: An obnoxious off-road vehicle.
BROOKIE: A disciple of Charlie Brooks.
EPHEMERELLA: A cocktail waitress at Mack's Bar, Butte, Mont.
DOUBLE HAUL: A casting technique utilizing two horses.

Think Kindly of the Worm

Let us, for a moment, consider the worm. Worms are good. They till the soil, recycling deceased vegetation. They are inoffensive neighbors, not given to noisy partying late at night. They are most cooperative, allowing their bodies to be used as fish teasers, affording youngsters entree to the magical realm of angling without having to memorize the Latin names of all those mayflies.

Worms can be faithful companions as well, and are easily trained in the social graces, i.e., proper table manners and the choice of an appropriate wine to go with Truite Cordon Bleu. The late Milford "Stanley" Poltroon had a soft spot (approximately the size of the Susan B. Anthony dollar) in his heart for worms, especially a pet nightcrawler called Wallace. This inseparable duo spent many a happy day fishing in Yellowstone Park disguised as periodontists from Cleveland. When Milf passed on to that great riffle in the sky (over Felt, Ida.) in '86, Wallace, heartbroken, moped for weeks, then threw himself under the wheels of a BMW. Greater love hath no worm.

In the esoteric world of fly fishers, the word "worm" is anathema, spoken in derision, often with a sneer of superiority toward those who would use them for catching trout. And a truly dedicated fly fisher would sooner be caught dealing coke, counterfeit twenties or used cars, than to be found possessing nightcrawlers with intent to fish. The purist insists on the challenge of artifice, imitating with feather and tinsel the mayfly, caddis, and midge, stone, and damsel, but never the worm, no.

Well, almost never. Scrounge through your fly box, especially the section devoted to nymphs, and I'll wager you'll find some extremely wormy-looking objects. Only a few have wormy names, like "Inchworm," "Rockworm," "Bloodworm," and the ubiquitous "Wooly Worm." Most are attempts to imitate the larval or pupal stages of

various insects, and them's worms, fellas. So let's not assume too much of a holier-than-thou attitude while drifting a big ol' Wooly Worm through that hole under the bank below the overhanging cedar with the "fly-fishing-only" sign on it.

We tend to forget that most of us got our first blooding in the fishbiz as little kids dangling worms in front of little fishes. Some, of course, have come later and older to embrace the fly, likely after giving up racquetball, hang gliding or golf, and thus never have experienced the exhilaration of watching the line twitch and move off as an eager fish inhales the worm.

I recall vividly my first trout from the tiny creek bordering my grandfather's farm. Hazel switch, length of cuttyhunk strong enough to tether a goat, snelled hook, and a lively red wiggler fresh from the manure pile. A shaded, brush-bound pool up against an ancient, barkless cedar log, domain of an alert, ferocious 7-whole-inch cutthroat, who savagely attacked the drifting worm, only to be snatched skyward and into the streamside vine-maple roots and skunk cabbage, there pounced upon by a grinning 6-year-old hollering "Grandpa, come see!"

From that moment I was irrevocably hooked. Even with the intervening sixty years, and a few sophistications of tackle and technique, when I am lucky enough to con a fish of noteworthy dimensions into taking my badly tied and ineptly presented fly, I am given to an enthusiastic whoop of unadulterated joy, much like the exultation of that 6-year-old over his first worm-caught trout.

Actually, we should be thankful for worms, even while we frown upon those who use them, and spend energy and perfectly good fishing time trying to convert them from their sinful ways. Though there still is a large body of worm dunkers, our prose-lytizing has resulted in an awesome increase in the numbers of fly fishers assaulting the lakes and streams. Where we once thought that persuading more and more people to become fly anglers would cut down on hubcap thievery, drug and wife abuse, and shopping-mall development, we now fear we have attracted more enthusiasts than our good fly-fishing waters can accommodate.

At least credit the angle worm for helping maintain a reasonable balance between stubborn worm drowners and righteous fly flingers, both caught somewhere in Ma Nature's weird food chain. As grandpa used to say, "Don't rock the wagon while you're in the middle of the creek," which I assumed to mean, be kind to worm fishers. And, for heaven's sake, don't keep that youngster from his first trout on a worm.

Streamside Etiquette

We have covered considerable distance and time in our approach to trout fishing since the days of rigidly enforced behavior on the English chalk streams, yet have managed to maintain at least some of the long-standing streamside manners bequeathed us by the sport's early practitioners. The increasing popularity of fly fishing, however, has flooded our rivers with a new generation of fishers, and these *nouveaux pecheurs* are often innocent of the niceties of the game. Perhaps unintentionally, they can be a disruptive influence to accustomed ritual. This notable falling-off of the old "brothers-of-the-angle" spirit, and the protocol once observed by all, has had dire consequences, alas.

It behooves us, therefore, to let this inexperienced and largely uninhibited group in on a few of the practices we traditionally hold dear, as well as to caution them about intrusive acts upon which we frown, or which may be hazardous to health. Appreciation of some of the nuances and unspoken rules of conduct might better prepare the neophyte for joining, relatively friction-free, us elders in our tradition-rich pursuit of trout on the fly. Otherwise, we may find it necessary to drop our normally open and friendly demeanor, and just throw them in the river.

Entering the Water

You should not join, willy-nilly, a line of anglers, such as steelheaders, working a stretch of stream. First ascertain which direction is "upstream," then move into line a comfortable distance above the uppermost fisherman, quietly. Cast patiently, taking pains not to foul-hook your immediate neighbor.

Move downstream only as they move. Don't push. Should you lose your footing, do not cry out or thrash about, but drift unobtrusively downstream until well clear of the others before attempting to regain your feet and composure. If you do not overly disturb the other anglers, you may even draw mild applause.

"You will be resented . . . if you should hook an ear other than your own."

"Despite all caution, one occasionally gets dunked."

The charms of angling

The charms of angling (Part II): Interesting wildlife.

(Part 1): pastoral meadows.

"Try to recapture your dignity as you flounder to beach or bank."

Matching the hatch (Part I).

Matching the hatch (Part II).

"I battled a dinner-plate-size crappie that thought it was a tarpon."

Matching the hatch (Part III).

"You should never join,

The charms of angling (Part III): Gentle breezes.

willy-nilly, a line of anglers."

"Overcasting another angler's line has led to a modest number of riverside homicides."

"Hmmm. I wonder what this trout has been feeding on."

Contentment is found in water close to home.

Casting

Always allow ample rod room to adjacent anglers when casting. Your technique and skill may be splendid and much to be admired, but will inevitably be resented if you infringe upon a fellow angler's air space. You will be resented even more if, with an inept cast, you should hook an ear other than one of your own.

Covering the Rise

Under no circumstance should you cover another angler's rise. It is considered in very bad taste. Fly fishers are normally non-violent and slow to anger, but overcasting another's line, or putting down his fish, has, on occasion, led to a modest number of riverside homicides, justifiable of course.

Wading

Right-of-way is recognized for its value toward pleasant angler relationships. The casual wader, intent on his progress, should never encroach upon a fellow fisher's water, i.e., the portion of stream he is fishing, or is about to fish. This is particularly true when he is casting to an actively rising trout. Long friendships have been dissolved over such actions, the young sternly admonished, and culprits rebuked in language dark and unadulterated. One thoughtless angler I have heard of had his waders badly perforated by a No. 16 Adams, and was advised not to return to the river until he had acquired better manners.

Do Fish Smell?

I don't relish seeing myths shattered, especially those about fishing. They add much to the romance and mystique of the sport. Oh, the old saws, "A wind from the south blows the bait in the fish's mouth," or "Bright day, bright fly, dark day, dark fly" (or is that the other way around?), still boast some validity on certain occasions. But we cling to a good many old sayings, even when disproven, just because they are nice myths, comfortable to fish by.

For instance, it is long established that fish smell. Whether by nostril, or lateral line, or by a tiny genetic microchip in their tiny brain, they can sniff out the one molecule in a billion of H20 that identifies their natal stream. That's pretty acute smelling, if you ask me. So I've always gone along with the idea that the smart angler doesn't go around fouling the waters with his sweaty hands, outboard fuel, or the residue of his peanut butter sandwich. Because the fishes can smell all that human-oriented gonk, are properly revolted, and will run like hell, that's why.

Now, along comes a video, titled *Why Fish Strike*, which I watched in awe the other night. It is a remarkable underwater expose of salmon chasing spoons, spinners, herring baits, and even flies, with varying degrees of curiosity and/or ferocity. Salmon were shown reacting to, approaching, and striking (or not) the various lures. One particular segment dealt with what happens when lures were given a thorough detergent bath to rid them of any human scent, or were treated to an attractor salve or lotion, or even dipped in nice oily bilge water. Here, according to the ancient view that fishes smell good, it follows that the salmon should have been attracted by the attractor-scented, repulsed by the bilge-dipped, and taken in completely by the squeaky-clean lure. Not so. Startlingly, the fishes largely ignored the tastily salved baits, paid nearly as little attention to the pristine lures, but greedily gobbled all of the "bilge-water specials." There goes the old "cleanliness" myth.

Except, maybe, for the matter of dipping your dirty pinkies in the fishes' water. Other studies have shown that human scent causes revulsion among trout and salmon, and a hand in the drink makes them scatter like trod-on quail. Washing the mitts doesn't remove enough of those bodily oils, and neither will the attempt to mask your aroma by squishing herring bait on the hands (or, for that matter, garlic, licorice or lite beer) have much effect.

Inventive local salmon fishers, perhaps hearing of the bilge water experiments, came up with an ideal cover-up for unwanted odors: WD-40 lubricant. The salmon seem to

approve, and the success ratio of WD-40-equipped anglers has notably improved. Also, the product can keep your tackle rust-free and your hands soft and supple.

A hesitant conclusion: All these many years trying to keep my aromas to myself and not on my tackle have been ill-spent. Fishes apparently are not turned off by my after shave, bug repellent, sun screen, lunch, or cigar smoke. Even my old outboard's contribution to the bilge is no longer as culpable as once thought. And dipping my flies in Jack Daniel's is a needless waste of good Tennessee sippin' whiskey.

Of course, I shall keep a few of the better myths operative. I'll "Fish up and fish fine" whenever the situation calls for it, and, naturally, I'll carry a can of WD-40.

Springtime = Trout

For dedicated fisherfolk, spring does not arrive officially until the opening of the trout season. Here in the Puget Sound country that means lowland lakes full of fat rainbows, eagerly awaiting their first spinner, egg, marshmallow, or fly. Tradition calls for a predawn gathering of troutsters, equally eager to shed the winter's dismals, flex their all-too-long unused fishing muscles, breathe the rich, outboard-perfumed air, and do battle with the wily trout.

With some exceptions, trout have not occurred naturally in our lakes for years, but are raised and trained in hatcheries, where they are taught to recognize the difference between Flatfish, Carey Specials, and green marshmallows, plus the comparative nutritional value of each. They also are schooled in techniques: When to bite, how to leap and struggle, and proper net behavior. Special attention is paid to learning to ignore the lures of self-styled "experts" in favor of baits dangled by inept but enthusiastic small children.

It is estimated that the average trout fisher, when pursuing his favorite quarry, carries approximately 46.2 pounds of tackle, not counting lunch and beer. Most of this gear is stored during the off-season in basements, closet shelves, and garages, and must somehow be located, untangled, de-rusted, and made operational the night before Opening Day. Fathers and grandfathers are responsible for seeing that nothing is missing upon arrival at the chosen lake. Kids are only responsible for bringing enthusiasm.

For fathers and grandfathers, Opening Day is a special moment for them to show off their outdoor talents and act as role models for their offspring. Like most predators, children must be taught the ways of nature, survival skills and, of course, how to catch fish. Some parents are better at this than others, but nearly all try to imbue the young with the underlying philosophy of fishing: Put a limit in the boat as fast as possible. A few emphasize conservation practices, but don't try to sell catch and release to a 6-year-old.

The boisterous crowds descending on the lakes hardly differ from those demonstrating for one socio/political cause or another, watching a football game, or attending a rock concert. Fisherfolk are mostly friendly and outgoing and, being unarmed, seldom given to open displays of barbarism. And all will lend a solicitous hand when someone falls overboard.

The atmosphere is festive: The rich aroma of burning hot dogs surmounts that of badly tuned outboards, the joyful screams of kids with hooked fish outbid the cries of hooked fathers and the keening of constantly starving youngsters. Despite normally abysmal weather, leaky boats, leaky rain gear, balky motors, broken tackle, soaked sandwiches, and cut fingers, fish are caught and memories made—rich memories of aching elder muscles and youthful laughter.

Fishfights

The fighting abilities of various fishes have long been debated, with debatable results. Steelhead, bass, sailfish, muskies, dorado, Atlantic salmon, bonefish, sculpin— all these have their champions. It all boils down to tackle, technique and attitude, and, personally, I don't give a large hoot. Whatever fish I happen to be pursuing at the moment is the ultimate battler.

I can be equally thrilled by the smashing strike of a steelhead in heavy water, the awesome cartwheels of an Atlantic salmon, the lip-smacking take of a nymphing "gulper," a largemouth engulfing a popping bug. And I have lucked into some awesome one-of-a-kind denizens: My first graphite rod was blooded on a ten-pound dogfish (I was after sea-run cutthroat). Jim Green, the rod's designer, still hasn't forgiven me.

I once hooked a large brown shark that cruised under the boat while we were fish-

ing for cohos off Cape Flattery, and watched as without any visible concern it continued its four-mile-an-hour course south. Ten-pound-test leader against a 300-pound juggernaut. I left the big streamer fly in its nose.

On a desert reservoir, I battled a dinner-plate-size crappie that thought it was a tarpon. And there was the Babine River steelhead that leaped over my skating mouse pattern in a clean miss, turned and rose again, missed, then chased the fly downstream for ten yards, back half out of the water, before crashing down on the helpless bug. Well remembered. Then there was the stupid cutthroat that rose to my jauntily drifting cigar butt.

Whatever is there in any given body of water, regardless of size, is my reward. They all fight their utmost, and are the trophies of the moment. I ask for no more.

Cutthroat Skiffing

Often, while crossing a Safeway parking lot or at a Costco exit, or even at First and Pike in downtown Seattle, I have been accosted by mature men, matrons or nubile young ladies, asking if I was Lucky Al, the semi-well-known cutthroat fisher, how I got started chasing sea-runs, and would I reveal all my secrets. Normally close-mouthed, I usually mumble "because they are there," as do mountaineers and hang-glider pilots.

Truthfully, I got mixed up with cutthroats inadvertently, being more a stream-bound trout and steelhead fisherman for uncounted years, favoring rock-hopping and wading swift currents. However, at one point, my feet quit on me, wading became more hazardous than usual, and trudging the bouldery streambeds became greatly painful, so I reluctantly resigned myself to a skiff and fishing a la butt.

Several of my fishing compatriots, among them Ed Foss, old cutthroat himself, claimed that sea-runs could be found off beaches and in estuaries here and also there on Puget Sound and Hood Canal. He even introduced me to a couple of beaches near Belfair, where I became hooked, or at least the learning process began.

After more than thirty years of this salty cutthroating, there still is much learning to be had, but I have arrived in the vicinity of several conclusions, none of which will help you a great deal in catching fish consistently. Cutts are not consistent. That's conclusion No. 1. They have also been regarded as "fall fish," pretty much following the salmon spawning runs. Baloney! (conclusion No. 2). I forget numbers 3, 4 and 5, but I have satisfied myself that most of the myths surrounding the mystical sea-run cutthroat can safely be ignored.

I have had some success exploring, just mooching a small streamer along a promising shore behind the oars. I favor, however, drifting along, casting toward (sometimes almost onto) the beach, and stripping in fast or faster, covering water from a foot to six or eight feet in depth. This can introduce you to cutts, or at least to weeds, flotsam, barnacled rocks, and assorted seafoods, like clams and oysters. Oysters are particularly fond of flies, striking viciously, often gumming leaders to shreds in their eagerness.

Beaches vary wildly in geography, from shallow mudflats through small gravel slopes to rough rocks and boulders, some with shell or weeds or both, or snags, pilings, or riprap, and sometimes piers and floats and moored cruisers. You name it, there can be cutts about. Though they can and do range considerable distances from their natal streams, they are often found near river and creek mouths. They seem to move around a lot, quite often in pairs or *menages-a-trois*, or *quatre* or worse. Hook one, stick around, maybe hook more.

Fortunately, cutthroats are not picky as to diet. Anything that moves is fair game, and will be attacked with vigor. Thus the angler's choice of fly patterns is quite broad, leaning heavily toward those simulating fry, candlefish, sculpin, small ducks and used condoms. Among my favorite attractors are the Cutthroat Yellow and Orange-Orange, which imitate the Cutthroat Yellow and Orange-Orange. I also rely on a green-over-white Candlefish tie, and occasionally a Muddler or a Sand Lance tube fly. And when I stumble onto rising fish I will switch my sink-tip for a floating line and a bushy buoyant dry fly to skate in front of the riser. The wets seem more consistent, though.

You also might run into a stray steelhead, especially near a stream mouth. I suspect that the steelies ask the cutts where the best lies and foodstuffs can be found, and the cutts gleefully point out the nearest unsuspecting fly angler's offering. I recall a fall trip to Belfair, where the Washington Fly Fishing Club had an eating, imbibing and incidental cutthroat-fishing outing at the state park. Just off the mouth of Mission Creek a number of us happened on a flotilla of steelhead, lazily roaming along a weedbed, and they seemed hardly perturbed by our lashings and flailings, nor the assorted flies zipping across their path. We hooked and lost many, and landed several before they became bored and headed elsewhere to spawn or whatever.

Where and when are cutthroats, you ask? I have spent many hours searching for them in the estuaries and along the shorelines, on all tides, in all weather. Many fishless days have accrued, but I have a few highly productive moments in memory, and have located a few favorite spots where the cutts seem to be cooperative. But I won't broadcast these places to just anyone. You'll have to find your own. Search often and patiently, as I did (and still do), for that bonanza beach. Don't look for me, though, for I'll likely be elsewhere, still searching.

Thumbs

I don't intend boring you with my infirmities, but I have this thing about thumbs. And thumbs are vital to the business of fly casting.

Arthritis has crept up on me, and my casting and fly-tying efforts have suffered. My thumbs hurt like hell. It's a lesson, you youngsters, in that you ought to enjoy your thumbs while you have their full cooperation. Mind you, I'm not preaching, or advocating a low-cholesterol, low-sodium or other low-whatever diet, but I do recommend keeping an eye on your thumbs.

There are many things you can do that don't require the use of a thumb: Eat a popsicle, point out someone's faults, hoist a martini, count up to four. But if you try to change a spark plug, wire a three-way light switch, tie a decent No. 16 Adams, or hitchhike without thumbs, you haven't a prayer. Or light a cigar on a cold, rainy cutthroat day.

Have I made my point? Respect your thumbs, yes.

Pike and Walleyes on Flies?

That was the question: Could walleyes and northern pike, not known as particularly good targets for the fly fisher, be taken with any consistency on flies? Could a couple of West Coasters, reasonably adept on trout and steelhead, find the fly patterns and techniques necessary for the catching? Resort owners, travel agents, and the Canadian Department of Tourism wanted to find out if the ever-expanding fly-fishing brigade might find happiness among pike and walleyes, the most popular game fishes across central Canada.

Thus Gil Nyerges and I found ourselves flying north out of Saskatoon to LaRonge, Saskatchewan, on the edge of the lakes country. From there the map, and the aerial view from the Cessna 185, showed a mosaic of lakes on every horizon. I swear half this province is water, and very little of it is accessible by road. As we flew northward for an hour, we could see fly-in fishing camps on a number of lakes, but most waters were barren of the human touch. But they were probably not barren of fish.

They were long, narrow lakes for the most part, many interconnected, and all somehow draining into the Churchill River and, ultimately and convolutedly, into Hudson Bay.

Landing between islands, we taxied down one of several narrow coves near the outlet of the middle of the three Foster Lakes. On a pine- and spruce-clad bench above the dock nestled Foster Lakes Lodge and its four cabins, where we were greeted by owner Trent Brunanski.

Brunanski's place was pretty sophisticated for a wilderness fish camp: Beds with daily changes of linen, hot showers, and a stocked refrigerator. At the lodge we delved into a gourmet buffet, while discussing walleyes, pike, and our fly-fishing hopes with Trent and a dozen other guests.

"How would these flies work on your pike?" I asked Trent, holding up a couple of huge garish patterns I had tied beforehand, monstrous versions of our sea-run cutthroat patterns. "I'll guess you'll either catch 'em or scare 'em over into Manitoba or clear down to Minneapolis," he said.

A cloudless dawn, a splendid breakfast, and we threw ourselves on the ministrations of Alex McKenzie, our Cree Indian guide, who allowed as how he could put us into the waters and weedbeds where Northerns were known to lurk. "Take 'em on flies?" he grinned. "You're nuts!" But he shrugged a good Indian shrug and said, "We can give it a try." It was a bit difficult for Gil and I to maintain our optimism in the face of all this skepticism, but we were determined to try.

We cruised uplake on fifteen mile-long Middle Foster until we reached an area of little coves and weedbeds where, according to Alex, Northerns were likely to be on the prod, and might even be susceptible to flies. He had a short spinning rod, rigged with a spoon the size of a banana, stashed back by the transom, and he said that was foolproof should we fail to catch our "lunch fish" on flies.

Dropping the anchor in eight feet of water on a reef extending out from a point, Alex waved toward the tules and said, "There's where they are." Gil and I unlimbered our artillery: Nine-foot rods, eight-weight sink-tip lines, short leaders with a foot-long, 25-pound tooth tippet, and size 1/0 Orange Oranges.

I could see the look of terror in Alex' eyes as I cast to port and Gil to starboard and our flies whistled past his head. But after we made a few dozen casts without lifting his cap even once, he seemed to relax.

I put a fair 60-foot cast out along the weedbed, let the fly settle to what I thought was a reasonable depth, then started a fast "cutthroat strip." Halfway to the boat there was a mottled flash as a two-foot-long pike lurched out of the weeds, yawned, and inhaled the fly. There was no need to set on him, for the big, barbless hook was well down in his gullet. Somewhat irritated, he took off to the northwest with vigor, which got him only about fifteen yards. He came back with some reluctance, rolled and thrashed his way around the boat, carefully eluding the anchor, then rolled into the net which Alex had artfully poked in his path. Then followed the ritual that was to become common: Alex donned heavy work gloves to grasp the pike by the eye sockets and poked a huge de-hooker down its gaping throat to retrieve my fly, then flopped the net over the side of the boat to release the fish. Off went the seven-pounder to his weedbed, hardly the worse for wear.

I won't claim the fishing was particularly fast, as we did considerable casting between takes, and we roamed a good many coves and weedy areas with only spotty action. Alex got a good deal more work hauling anchor than he did with the net. Nevertheless, he allowed that "you're doing pretty good. The party I had out yesterday only landed three fish for the day, trolling, and you fellas have already hooked a dozen." With that plaudit Gil and I, now somewhat relaxed, proceeded to hook a pair of five-pounders for lunch.

This is where Alex really earned his keep, and our admiration, as he expertly filleted the pike for our main course. Ashore he gathered an armload of birch twigs and branches, set up the grill he had stashed in the boat, and brought out the chuck box with its assortment of pots, a huge iron skillet, and packets of vegetables for salad. All this, with appropriate gestures, led to a splendid repast, but made getting back to serious fishing something of a labor.

We cruised on farther up the lake to finish out the afternoon, winding through a maze of small, timbered islands and an assortment of intriguing coves. An eagle soared from a piney bluff near the inlet stream from Upper Foster Lake, where we drifted just off the mouth. Heavy weeds just under the surface here said "pike water," and that was what came to our flies. We learned that a seven-pounder can pick up and tow around seemingly a ton of weeds before giving up to the net. We caught several, then went ashore, put on our waders, and explored the enticing river. Gil teased up some miniature something or others, whether pike fingerlings or whitefish we never did find out, but nothing catchable as we had hoped. So we returned to the boat, and the pike.

Heading back toward camp, we dropped into a number of promising, weed-rimmed coves, all sheltered from the afternoon's stiffening wind. In nearly every one there was a pike, sometimes two, and they did seem a bit more ferocious and challenging in a confined area, especially with weeds, lily pads, and a few formidable snags. Netting and releasing Gil's last, a weed-wrapped eight-pounder, Alex said, "My netting arm is getting tired, time to head for supper." Later, across the well-laid table, Trent said, "OK, you've exercised the pike enough. Tomorrow we'll fly up to Hodges Lake, where you can try your flies out on the walleyes."

One of the delightful disadvantages of most fishing resorts is that they feed too well. Those of us who have calorie-counting wives are presented with a tantalizing variety of foods, each meal causing a momentary pang of conscience. Recklessly we indulge and enjoy, saying, "I'll catch up with the old diet later, yes." Certainly a satisfied stomach starts the fishing out right, but can make the first dozen or so casts rather lethargic. A rough life, indeed.

Brunanski flew us north for an hour, heading for Hodges, the walleye lake, over a confusing lakescape, with seemingly hundreds of lakes in every direction. Navigation here is a matter of recognizing this lake by its odd shape, or that one by its islands, or another by the charred snags of an old forest fire. We passed one landmark, a section of river, connecting two long lakes, a stretch of broken water with several falls and rapids, noted for grayling and rainbows, but flew on to land on Hodges, near an abandoned mining camp. On the shore was a 14-foot outboard skiff, which would afford us transport around the lake in search of likely walleye waters.

We cruised islands, weedbeds, and reefs, anchoring here and there to cast over promising fishy spots, and probed numerous coves. Again, there were pike all over to keep us busy, from juveniles to ten-pounders, greedy for our varied bright bucktails. Feeling that perhaps we were not fishing deep enough for the walleyes, I switched from the sink-tip line to a full high-density sinking line, as did Gil. Minutes later, as we mooched along a rocky shoreline, he had a more vigorous strike, a wild run and jump, and the flicker of a white-edged fin. No pike, this, but a nice three-pound walleye, with appreciably more battle in him than the fish we had been catching. Shortly after, and within yards of that first one, I hooked my first walleye, a stubborn three-jumper, that gave me a respectable rainbow-like tussle before coming to net. Apparently we were in a favored walleye locale, for we managed to lose several more until failing daylight forced us to quit for the flight back to the lodge. But we had at least proved to ourselves that walleye could be conned into taking flies.

After another gourmet meal, we had a fireside chat in the lodge with Trent and Alex, our guide, as to what we might try on our last morning. We had hoped to find some lake trout coming up out of their normal deep-water habitat into the outlet stream of Middle Foster, not far from camp, so we elected to give that a try. Next morning we boated to the head of the river, then hiked the quarter-mile down to Lower Foster.

There Alex and I took the skiff, while Gil launched his float tube and headed down the inlet channel. In a good flow of current we cast over the shallows, and caught . . . you guessed it . . . pike. No lakers, no walleyes, just pike, but surprisingly better fighters in the moving water. We released maybe a dozen apiece before we had to return to camp for lunch and the inevitable fly-out.

You might term it "mission accomplished," for we proved to a skeptical Cree guide—and to ourselves—that pike and walleye will take flies. It is not likely that Alex is now a convert to fly fishing, but at least he can talk a good and broader game to future clients. The Canadian tourist and travel folk also will be pleased to add fly fishing for these fishes to their already broad attractions. So to pike and walleye, wherever found, beware that colorful, tinseled, hairy, feathered monstrosity coursing erratically past your nose; it may have a hook in it.

Fly Tying

Fly tying is a pastime unto itself—often an angler becomes so engrossed in it that his fishing time is seriously curtailed.

Not me. I started tying my own flies only when I became disenchanted with the ones I had been using, tied on hooks with gut snells about four inches long and a knobby loop on the end. My ten-year-old mind—for that's how old I was then—opined that snelled flies were a bit awkward and likely to offend any self-respecting trout. So I began fashioning flies on No. 10 worm hooks, with ring eyes big enough to stuff a 10-pound-test leader through if necessary. An ancient Hardy catalog of my grandfather's provided illustrations of patterns, to which I made many substitutions and obvious improvements, depending on what materials I had available.

Mostly I relied on a Rhode Island rooster's neck, which I plucked often, much to his annoyance. Mother's knitting basket was raided for various colored yarns. A vise was concocted from a pair of pliers anchored to a wood block, and tensioned by a heavy rubber band. The flies that came from this contraption were mostly brown and crudely lumpy, but many a trout and crappie mistakenly considered them edible, to their chagrin. In time the flies would improve somewhat.

There was a little bay a mile walk down the railroad tracks from our house, just below the hill where the University of Washington dominated the landscape. The reedy shoreline was incised by numerous little sloughs and channels, just the proper size for a fly rod if one could step through the tules and find a non-sinking spot in the peat to stand and cast. Leachate from the slag pile below the university's electric generating plant gave the waters a weak decaf color and lent a nose-twitching acidic aroma to the whole area. Nearby was the shell house, where the U.W. rowing crew launched their racy craft before heading out onto Lake Washington. Blackbirds and an assortment of water-oriented varmints made their calls and splashes, but otherwise it was a peaceful if not exactly pristine place. I frequented it often, to see if my latest fly-tying experiment would be eagerly accepted by the local denizens: trout, kokanee, crappies, perch, and an occasional bass.

Naturally, at that tender age, I also carried a tobacco tin of worms and a few chamois strips, just for insurance. It was a great place for a youngster to hone his fishing skills, and incidentally, sometimes bring home much appreciated protein. There are campus buildings there now, a ball field and a monstrous parking lot. There are still blackbirds, but not many fish or fishers. Progress.

Later I tied flies while working in my uncle's hardware store in Oregon. The term "working" was taken rather lightly, as I was more interested in fishing than work. I sold a few nails, barbed wire, and shovels, but it was obvious I was not cut out for merchandising. My uncle Ray put up with me mainly because I could talk fishing with the locals, and tie flies, mostly Gray Hackles and red salmon trebles, which satisfied the immediate demands.

I was also a mainstay on the local softball team, hitting .350 against the CCC boys, and assorted timber and farm squads in the Forest Grove area. It was a nice athletic summer, but I failed to improve the cash flow of the store, and was paid accordingly. Actually I ate a good deal more than I was worth, but the Gray Hackles and the fishing were certainly noteworthy.

I still tie flies, but only to satisfy my own needs and fill up the empty squares in my fly boxes. And I don't allow it to curtail my fishing time.

Local Fishing

Next to having an English butler, a French cook, and a harem, having a good trout water within reasonable driving distance makes life worth living. Most of us make do with a delightful, loving, hard-working, long-suffering wife, and a ten-year-old pickup that can make it, with luck, to the nearest fishing spots.

Keeping on amicable terms with your fishing widow takes many skills: plumbing, gardening, repairing small engines and appliances, moving furniture, reaching high shelves, painting stuff, even cooking, all taking up valuable fishing time, but necessary in building points toward time off for pursuit of fishes.

There are places where a fly fisher can be almost guaranteed of success. Most of them are in Alaska, New Zealand, Argentina, and other selected waters at least half an ocean and a good many bucks away. In these places almost anyone with a fly rod and rudimentary skills can become an instant expert, returning to the real world to brag of awesome catches to envious friends of equal ineptitude but thinner checkbooks. Nevertheless, with but few exceptions, I have been content with waters closer to home (and within a newspaperman's exchequer) where the fishing is, at best, sketchy, dominated by pan-size trout, with an occasional steelhead or salmon thrown in.

This is not all bad, understand, for the sport more often than not is a true challenge, not only of skill, but of patience, fortitude, and the idea that trophy trout are less of an end product than the fishing itself. Even so, I still carry the lurking thought

that the next cast might cause a reckless fish of awesome dimensions to rise to my badly presented fly. Fortunately, it happens—not often, of course, but there are moments of glory.

This philosophy has been passed down by each generation of fishers to the next. I pass it now to you, with a warning that it is essentially all baloney, but necessary baloney, to persuade you that fishless days are just as good as fishy ones.

I won't lie to you. I hate to be skunked. That goes for local waters as well as Argentina and New Zealand.

The Poltroon Connection

I first met Milford "Stanley" Poltroon in a wastebasket, which, in hindsight, seems appropriate.

The wastebasket belonged to Enos Bradner, and he had just swept into it the top layer of junk mail from his desk. Among the items was an early copy of *The Wretched Mess News*, a little fishy periodical that was mailed to outdoor writers, among others. Bradner was on the mailing list as outdoor editor of *The Seattle Times*, where I was employed as a staff artist. I had known and fished with Brad for a dozen years, and often left my drawing board to wander down the hall and lean on his desk to talk fish, flies, and whatever was happening on the North Fork of the Stillaguamish, his favorite steelhead river.

As I fished the copy of *The Wretched Mess News* out of Bradner's wastebasket, he exclaimed "Trash!" Trash it admittedly, even boastfully, was, claiming to be "the last stronghold of fearless yellow journalism" and seeking to "bring culture into your formerly drab existence." But after closer inspection, the satire of its editor, Milford Poltroon, clutched my vulnerable brain (see "Do You Have a Brain?" somewhere up front in this very book). Somewhat to Brad's disgust—"I don't understand this," he said, but he was always saying that—I was hooked, and forthwith wrote Poltroon for "more information." Thus began a chain of cataclysmic events which would change my otherwise culture-free life, my fishing, my artistic career, my dietary habits, and a host of other vital functions.

More information arrived shortly: a large carton containing a grand assortment of oddities, including coupons for dog food, chits for a Las Vegas Faro table, an outdated offer for a half-price stay in Fiji, several arty posters for Parisian shows, a nice inflatable fish, a genuine stale peanut-butter sandwich, an armload of styrofoam "76" balls, chits for free beers at an obscure saloon, a 1930 Sears Catalog, tear sheets from several fishing magazines, and a quarter mile of tangled monofilament (twenty-pound test). The cover letter, hand-scrawled, said: "If you wish further information send money, preferably in large, untraceable bills." It was signed, shakily, "Milf."

Appropriately impressed with this personalized service, I quickly wrote for a subscription, but enclosed no money. On a lowly newspaperman's salary (something like $47 per week), there was no way I could justify the extravagance of a magazine that cost a dollar ($1) a year. However, I did send along a hand-drawn original fishy cartoon, worth, on the local open-air art market, maybe a buck and a quarter, which would allow a little slack for dickering.

Almost on the next post came a copy of *The Wretched Mess News*, plus a letter. "My art appraiser, Leonardo Poltroon, says he likes your stuff, but you still owe me about two bits," it said. "I will be in Seattle, wherever that is, on Wednesday next. Lunch with me. Discuss stuff: art, fish, sex, the double-haul, other heavy stuff. Yes. Milf."

And so it came to pass that we met eyeball-to-eyeball. Well, maybe not quite, for Milford "Stanley" Poltroon was only 3 or 4 hectares in height, and his resplendent beard barely brushed my sternum. But he sported a matched set of piercing blue eyes, ears that would be the envy of any Ubangi warrior, and a necktie graphically depicting Washington crossing the Delaware, or Potomac, or some other trout stream. His real name was Dave Bascom, and when he wasn't being Milford Poltroon he worked at an advertising agency in San Francisco.

Over lunch we discussed fishy philosophies, fly patterns, Jack Daniel's, forestry practices, Greek mythology, hatchery vs. wild trout, and found much common ground and water. I concluded that if Milford had been born centuries earlier, he likely would have invented the double haul and written both Dame Juliana's *Treatysse* and Walton's *Compleat Angler*, and both would have been funnier. He wouldn't have cared much for the life of those days, however, even with the trout fishing then available, because peanut butter, his favorite food and basic protein source, had yet to be conceived.

Milford's recognition of me as a kindred spirit led to his offering me a job at the ad agency, at 2X what I was making at *The Times*. I disrespectfully declined, but allowed as how I would like to contribute to *The Wretched Mess News* in one capacity or another.

"Great!" Milford exclaimed. "I shall appoint you Litter and Pollution Editor, in lieu of remuneration, and you will henceforth have all the perks and power the title holds, yes." The perks were impossible to pass up: Air fare (one way) to West Yellowstone, Montana, where Poltroon had a summer cabin, free beer, unlimited parking at the cabin, and ready access to Montana's highly reputed fly fishing. Thus occurred my absorption into *The Wretched Mess* and the Poltroon family.

The Poltroons, it turned out, were mainly Milford "Stanley" and an assortment of oddballs who used the same name, i.e., Harriet Beecher Poltroon, Milford's wife, who doubled as Sex & Garden Editor; J. Lasker Poltroon, Advertising Manager; Sneakers Poltroon, Financial Editor; Roberta Poltroon, Cooking & Garbage Editor; and Billy Grahamcracker (a Poltroon once removed), Religion & Bingo Editor, all of whom were subject to immediate dismissal if they failed to conform to Milford's baser standards.

This auspicious staff produced *The Wretched Mess*, a more or less quarterly publication aimed at outdoorsy types, especially fly fishers, tree toppers, beer salesman, beer drinkers, appliance repairfolk, orthopedic surgeons, hang-glider pilots, fry cooks, and the like. Subscribers were legion (American Legion, French Foreign Legion, Legion of Disbarred Attorneys, etc.) and the *Mess* reached around the globe, with copies appearing in Cyprus, Tasmania, the Maldives, and Pocatello.

As the first truly meaningful use of movable type, the *Mess* left an indelible mark,

not unlike the sooty fingerprints on your guest towels. It was born one overly humid day when Milford decided that a publication dedicated to "culture through satire" would appeal to the literati (that is, fly fishers), create new T-shirt designs, and make him large quantities of money, allowing him to forsake the penury of the advertising business and pursue his paramount interests—fishing, having sex while fishing, and, when not actively engaged in either of the above, just plain thinking about fishing (this is the longest single sentence you will find in this book, and I hasten to apologize, although it does have a nice lilt, you must admit. You can blame it, in part, on my word processor, which, now ten years old, has taken on some irrational and prankish habits, slipping in excess commas, garbled syntax and whimsical spellings).

Poltroon arrived at fly fishing rather late in life, but being a quick study he immediately learned all there is to know about the subject. The *Wretched Mess* gave him a podium from which he could launch attacks on angling myths and pomposities, the Forest Service, the Army Corps of Engineers, worm dunkers, state fish and game departments, and the furbish lousewort. The magazine also stressed education, publishing many splendidly informative articles, such as "How to Build A Bluegill-Resistant Hygrometer," "How to Play Fish (musically)," "How to Store Pike in Your Pianoforte," and "How to Cheat."

Though the *Wretched Mess* was a blatant satire of "normal" outdoor publications, it had its own unique patina, possibly due to spilled beer or dry-fly floatant. It also was devoted to angling trivia not found in any other publication. Where else could you be offered facts like "the Leaning Tower of West Yellowstone actually is vertical, while the town itself leans approximately 12 degrees (Celsius) to the southeast, due to a rather capricious tectonic plate shift near Macks Inn, Idaho"?

In addition to being editor, publisher and head creative genius, Milford also handled the advertising, concocting and printing all the ads without any say-so whatsoever from the advertisers. Poltroon claimed he knew a good ad when he saw one, and to hell with you, Charley. Advertisers were often shocked when they saw their ads in print, but they were universally pleased with the responses, including a few (rare) ecstatic advertisers who said they received more than $600 return from each dollar spent.

For the most part, the ads were superior to the editorial content of the magazine, and

Milford Poltroon.

63

considerably funnier. If an ad failed to "sell" adequately, Milf would quickly fire one or another of the Poltroons appearing on the masthead, then reappoint them under a new title. I myself suffered changes from Indoor Editor to Outdoor Editor to Assistant Music Critic and finally back to Litter and Pollution Editor, my final resting place.

It was a heart-warming association, and one which necessitated my occasional presence at Milford's estancia (read hut) on Hebgen Lake, outside West Yellowstone, where we created and glued together the *Mess* and its famed sister publication, The *Wretched Mess Calendar;* consumed much beer and disported on the many great trout waters close by.

Usually I would go there every spring after snowmelt, not only to work on the *Mess* but also to help open Milford's cabin for the season. Two weeks would be spent turning on the water system and the gas and chasing out the bats, marmots, and mice that had homesteaded the place over the winter. Consuming great gourmet repasts, consisting mainly of garlic (an excellent mosquito repellent), we would strive to create an issue or two of the *Mess* while still reserving ample morning and evening time to pursue local fishes. It was often difficult for us to choose among the "blue-ribbon" streams available on which to cast our flies, including the Madison, Gallatin, Firehole, and Henry's Fork, but we somehow managed.

Of course, we also had to consort occasionally with local experts Bud Lilly, Bob Jacklin, Pat Barnes, Charlie Brooks, and Cal Dunbar in order to assure we were fishing the right waters. This often paid off. In one memorable instance, Milf and I asked about the prospects on Duck Creek. Consensus was that the Duck was still high and dirty, nobody was fishing it, and there were grizzlies afoot in the valley. Forget it, they said. So we went to Duck Creek. Sure, it was well up on its banks, the color of coffee mocha, there was reasonably fresh bear scat on the path, and it was obvious a thundershower was threatening.

Milford's first cast with a large Muddler resulted in a huge (anywhere from 3 to 22 pounds) brown trout that ripped out 40 feet of WF7S line before severing his six-pound-test leader on an inappropriately placed snag. I managed to break a like-sized denizen on a Wooly Worm, then land a three-pounder. Thus it went, fish after fish for an hour, as the rain thickened. We landed and released a dozen each and lost others until we ran out of Wooly Worms.

Momentarily sheltered under a pine, Milf suggested I tie up some more Woolies while we had a beer. None of the few materials I dug from my vest were particularly Wooly Worm-like, but I located a spare plastic shoestring, from which I crafted a highly nutritious-looking body, and palmered it with a luscious webby brown hackle. With the tag end of the plastic shoestring hanging out, it looked something like a juvenile lobster, a wounded beaver, or something equally edible. We christened it Poltroon's Passion. I tied two. The Duck Creek browns took to it like cat to nip, and we rounded out the afternoon with a brace of four-pounders before the storm chased us back home.

There is no moral to this story, as trout—especially those in Duck Creek—are all highly immoral. But later that season the Poltroon's Passion was declared illegal on Yellowstone Park waters.

Milford was always a perfect host, no matter who his guests were. He entertained myriad anglers, without regard to race, creed, or sexual persuasion, providing they could chop firewood and wash dishes with reasonable dexterity. He also provided personalized guide service to his favorite fishing spots, many of which boasted large, frequently cooperative trout.

One year I had companions Ed Foss and Vince Sellen with me on our way to the Federation of Fly Fishers conclave in West Yellowstone, and persuaded Poltroon to offer us bed and board at his Hebgen estancia. After lengthy conversations and consumption of a reasonable amount of Jack Daniel's, Milf allowed as how he thought these two could be trusted on one of his favored fishing holes. Thus we set out in Milf's venerable Moosewagen, a 1954 Volkswagen bus replete with antlers and a tail, for the noted patch of water on the South Fork of the Madison known as Mollie's Nipple.

Now in order to get to Mollie's from Poltroon's place, one must head south to the highway, five miles, then west a piece, then north another five miles down the opposite bank to arrive but a stone's throw from whence one started. Not only did this seem silly, but time was of the essence if we were to make the five o'clock hatch, so Milf called for a shortcut. I, as Moosewagen guest pilot, obeyed, lurching off the graveled main road onto a barely discernible cattle track. Great, water-filled ruts of questionable depth were surmounted as the Moosewagen groaned and slewed for a mile until we reached a locked gate. Milf produced a key and waved us through onto a cattle ranch.

Another mile onward, with cab-high sagebrush whacking the windows, Ed was prompted to ask, "Do you know where you're going?" Just then Milf shouted, "Hang a left here, Alport!" I did so, even though there was no apparent opening in the brush, much to the discomfort of our already shaken passengers. A number of chuck holes later we arrived at a bare patch in the sage. "We are arrived!" Milford cried, and we dismounted and had a beer while donning waders and rigging up rods. Although we couldn't see anything through the sage, we could hear the sound of running water, which meant we were somewhere in the vicinity of Mollie's.

We hiked a few hundred feet down a hill, broke out into a semi-meadow, waded a tiny little feeder creek, and presto, fishing water ahead. The sun was low behind us, a slight breeze wiggled the streamside grasses, and, sure enough, the hatch was in progress, with numerous rises dimpling the surface. Sounds of slurping trout smote our ears. For an hour, until the air took on its post-sunset chill, we cast to rising fish, hooked many, lost scores, released awesome numbers, rainbows and browns from a foot to three pounds, and ubiquitous squaw fish, some of which we kept, at Milf's request, for smoking. It was a gratifying time, and Ed and Vince gave Milf a seated ovation, while getting out of their waders. The trip back to the cabin seemed less lumpy.

To top the evening off, Poltroon, with his usual flourishes, concocted a splendid supper, complete with a fine, screw-cap Sauvignon Blanc. And we did the dishes, with Ed saying, "When I die, I want to die here, after a day like this with Milford Poltroon!"

No finer accolade to a great host can be made. But Milf had already gone to bed.

The Wretched Mess survived for thirteen years, almost profitably, before it became obvious that it was cutting too deeply into our fishing time, and that it either must go "big time," with the attendant increase in staff, expenses, postage, and more beer, or be bagged while still at its nadir. To the relief of all other outdoor publications, the board of directors (all Poltroons) adjourned to the banks of Yellowstone's Firehole River where, at the height of the Nutragena hatch, we elected to kill *The Wretched Mess* while we were still of a piece, ambulatory and near-solvent.

Having contributed so little to Post-Colombian culture, I would like to be remembered as Al Poltroon, Litter & Pollution Editor of *The Wretched Mess News*, yes, with perhaps a suitable epitaph scratched on that boulder I kept tripping over on the South Fork.

"Here lies Al," it would say, "just a stone's throw from that Big Mother Brown Trout he caught on a size eighteen Adams at this spot." Yes.

Renew Spirits and Solve Global Problems

Every so often I catch myself worrying about major global affairs like potential polar ice-cap melt, the shrinking Amazonian rain forest, and static cling. When this happens I feel it's time to take stock, tackle, and go fishing.

To some this may seem to be copping out, but I've found that a day away from these traumatic issues can be quite rewarding, and I return (even fishless) rejuvenated and capable of tackling those problems with renewed vigor and often innovative solutions. There's nothing like the friendly environs of a trout stream to dissipate urban stresses, clear the sinuses, and cause corpuscles to move around less sluggishly and brain cells to function in more orderly fashion.

I recall with satisfaction resolving the urban gang problem, shortly after persuading a nice rainbow to forsake his bouldery hideaway and nail my artfully drifted Elk-hair Caddis. The answer to gangs, I assayed, would be to divert their attention from vandalism, drive-by shootings, and unsafe sex and put them to more positive pursuits, such as stream renewal. But I haven't yet figured out how to persuade a leather-jacketed, pistol-packing, 200-pound teenager to give up his thuggish habits for a shovel and a wet day on a snag-cluttered creek. I'm not sure a passionate discourse on the desirability of improving the environment will have the desired affect. Perhaps a Crocodile Dundee approach—"Now that's not a knife, THIS is a knife"—will do it.

Aphorisms to Fish By

When the going gets tough, I usually quit.
What's good for General Motors is good for General Motors.
When interest rates go down so does my interest.
Keep your fishing vehicle in fresh oil and it will run forever.

Floating Craft

Beyond the creeks, small rivers and beaver ponds, you will find many waters that are just not wadeable. Lakes, bays, large rivers, sounds, and estuaries require some kind of floating device as either a fishing platform or for transport.

Every marine contraption, from cruiser to skiff to float tube, has its necessary moments. Actually, the number of craft a dedicated angler owns depends on his wallet and storage space in his garage or back yard. For example, I am not unusual in that I have a 16-foot inboard/outboard rigged for Puget Sound salmon, a 12-foot plywood jon boat with a 4-horsepower outboard for sea-run cutts, an 8-foot aluminum pram for lakes, a float tube, waders, and a flotation vest. Needless to say, they take up considerable acreage, but I am equipped for most any angling foray that strikes me.

I don't own a McKenzie drift rig, probably the most efficiently designed river boat ever made, and pretty, but I rely on friends and guides so equipped. However, you can make do with a modest cartopper, and go on from there as your exchequer dictates. I started with a canvas kayak as a kid and caught fish.

But I'm not about to show up on my favorite sea-run estuary in a twin-outboard, metal-flake, radar-guided, fish-findered, high-tech, 50-mph bass boat—although it might be fun.

Who Invented Fly Fishing?

Though I've been told differently, I like to think fly fishing was invented by the Scots. The sport seems to fit the Scottish stereotype of thrift, frugality, and conservative demeanor. Obviously it was more economical to utilize otherwise wasted feathers from fowl, which, lashed to hooks, were reusable for fysshe after fysshe, whereas bait, such as cheese eggs, marshmallows, etc., was good only for a single strike.

Face it, the Scots, like present-day fly fishers, were cheap, cheap, cheap. Remember, they were the ones who introduced the kilt, to save material that could have been made into trousers. They favored horsehair leaders and greenheart rods, made of indigenous materials instead of exotic imported bamboo and boron. They eschewed high-tech innovative tackle, like the sonar fish finder and the shooting head, and were absolutely livid over even the thought of Flashabou or fluorescent yarn on their flies. No Scot, so far as I can determine, has ever set foot in a jet boat, let alone fished from one.

The Scots did, however, provide us with some enduring fly patterns: The Partridge and Puce, Teal and Magenta, Snipe & Blae, Glenlivet and Aqua, for which we are grateful.

Companions

I am blessed with a coterie of fly-fishing friends who, despite knowing me quite well, still invite me to fish with them, or, should I entreat them to join me, do not invent semi-transparent excuses for urgent, irrevocable commitments elsewhere.

This choice group has all the attributes I deem vital for ideal companionship. They must speak English, share my taste in Bach and sons and Tennessee sippin'

whiskey, be unoffended by my cigars, and tie flies which I can borrow. It's nice if they can cook. I'll even put up with the fact that most are better fishermen than I, but are able to stifle their comments on my casting.

One such favored companion is Steve Raymond, author of splendid fish tales, fly tier of excellence, knowledgeable of flora, fauna, and things political and piscatorial, and the only truly competent side-arm caster I know short (by only a few feet) of Lefty Kreh. We have shared many convivial hours on various slippery-rocked rivers, wind-buffeted estuaries, and mosquito-swarmed lakes, as well as beach-side campfires where the world's travails were, semi-effectively, solved.

Another of my closest friends and fellow fishermen is Bill Rundall, one of those men whose troubles seem to be more than any single person's allotment. He's a droll gent, smiles a lot, and never have I heard a discouraging word from him, nor a bellyache about his vicissitudes.

Bill is dogged by Murphy's Law. A good fisher, Bill can lose the unloseable fish, break a rod tip, knock his Thermos overboard, flood his outboard, or the skiff. If there is anything to trip over, it will be in Bill's path. Folding chairs collapse when he sits, perfectly sound trees disintegrate at his touch, and rocks roll fretfully beneath his feet. All in all Bill is, yes, accident-prone.

Perhaps his greatest mischance was the time he completed a fairly travail-free fishing trip, arriving home unscathed, and disembarked from his trusty carryall to open the garage door. Silhouetted in the headlights, Bill noted with apprehension that the truck was moving inexorably toward him down the inclined driveway. In a trice, or five seconds, whichever came first, two tons of International Harvester pinned Bill against the door, leaving a reasonably accurate Rundall impression in the wood. In the following recuperative months, Bill got rid of the accursed carryall and masochistically bought a Pinto.

No words about fly fishing would be complete without some mention of Enos Bradner, the much-revered sage of Northwest angling. In the early '40s he ran a little bookstore in Seattle, belonged to the Steelhead Trout Club, founded the Washington Fly Fishing Club, and fished a lot, especially on the North Fork of the Stillaguamish.

I first met Brad at Haury's Boathouse, where *The Seattle Times*, for whom I worked, was sponsoring a salmon derby. Enos was one of the judges, along with Mel Sayre, then sports editor of *The Times*, who had asked me along as an observer. Bradner, sensing that I had the proper requisites of eagerness and innocence to be a potential Washington Fly Fishing Club member, invited me to attend the club's monthly meeting, where I would rub casting arms with some of the local notable fly fishers. This I did, but failed to join, for Uncle Sam snatched me off to the war (World War II, that was my war, three-and-a-half years' worth).

When I returned to *The Times* in '45 I found Bradner had been made outdoor editor of the paper, with his desk just down the hall from the art department where I was chained. There being no other fly fishermen in the newsroom at that time, it was inevitable that Brad and I would become good friends, and we shared many convivial angling exploits.

Good fortune has provided me with other pleasant fishing companions, but these were three of the best.

Cussing

I have known and admired a number of the great cussers of our time, especially those who laid their colorful curses upon recalcitrant fishing gear, reluctant fishes, or their own casting ineptitudes. But one hero emerges.

This was fellow newsman Bob Barr, a *Seattle Times* reporter whose rich vocabulary of obscenities was apparently limitless. His conversations were punctuated by epithetica rarely found in Webster's. But in mixed company or the presence of malleable children, his language was carefully edited, and came out as high-order English, as did his writing

reportage. Yet he could, when confronted by a bad cast or a missed strike, fry a leader or stun a rising trout with his invective.

Once I witnessed his harangue of a large mid-stream rock that had interfered with his attempts to cover a rising brown trout; he assaulted the rock with a laser-like stream of profanity. This was typical, for his robust adjectives were mainly directed at inanimate objects, like snags, boulders, streambank bushes, boots, hats, etc., but occasionally also reached out to encompass fish, birds, elk, mosquitoes, and passing worm fishers.

Despite his brusque and brutal use of language, Barr was compassionate and inwardly as soft as old-fashioned oatmeal, and he could, as a reporter, ingratiate himself equally with mugging victims, crying children, or treed cats.

Gramps

Shortly out of diapers I developed an obsession for water. I blame it on genetics and environment more or less equally. Both grandfathers contributed.

In the case of one I was the only grandson, and in the other I was the eldest, thus I was blessed with the best efforts of both to develop in me a full appreciation of the part fishes play in a boy's life and a man's lifetime. Thanks to them I have had a long

and rewarding career of fish chasing, coupled with a respect bordering on awe for the environs in which fishes disport. I was also utterly ruined from becoming a responsible, productive member of society, for which I am duly appreciative.

One grandfather, Gramp Chilcote, Dutchman, farmer, and all-around woodsman, showed me how wood was cut, cows milked, hay stacked and, incidentally, how to catch the little trout in Cedar Creek, which ran through his Yacolt stump ranch, on angle worms of course. I spent many a summer with a fresh-cut hazel rod, gut leader and snelled hook, poking through the vine-maple thickets, trying to entice the fast and furtive native cutthroats from their shadowed brush piles, with considerable success.

Occasionally my other grandfather, Gramp Pratt, an optometrist, would visit from Portland and entice me away from the barnyard to explore the creek's headwaters, less brushy and more suited to the fly fisher, which he was. Here he showed me the basics of fly fishing, entrusting me with a three-piece bamboo rod, soaked gut leader, and assorted dry flies, mostly Brown Hackles and Blue Uprights he had tied himself.

Gramp Pratt taught me how to cast to pockets in the boulder-studded creek, how to doctor a fly with anise oil to make it float more appetizingly where the little cutthroats lurked, and how to quickly set the hook on the speedy little buggers—but not so quickly as to break the fragile gut. It was there I hooked my first sizable trout, a behemoth of 13 inches which called on all my juvenile skills, plus my first taste of "fisherman's luck" to land, but I finally pounced on it in the shallows, and heaved it mercilessly onto the bank. I was broken forever from the hazel switch and the angle worm.

Even when we moved to Alki Point in West Seattle, I spent many happy if mostly unproductive hours attempting to entice local fishes to the fly. Bullheads responded. All this led to a lifetime dominated by the unrelenting urge to cast a line into every piece of water, fresh or salt, moving or placid, suspected of containing fishes. Even now, after more than 60 years of fishing, I still look with anticipation at any passing creek or puddle. They all look fishy to me.

My father, a casual fisherman at best, never quite fathomed my obsession with trout fishing, though somewhat reluctantly allowed as how it was perhaps a better pastime then baseball, football, hockey or chasing nubile young ladies, pursuits I dabbled in occasionally during my teens. Always it seemed, I held fishing in higher priority. Thus our Sunday family outings and vacations somehow ended up on bodies of water containing fishes, or the prospect thereof.

Gradually I became more knowledgeable about fishes, tackle and technique, to the point where I could return home, head held high, with a reasonably full creel. This was back in the days when a limit catch of trout was twenty and the criterion for gauging your success as an angler, whether you ate them or gave them away. We all went through that period of arrogance, proudly proclaiming limit catches, until realizing that the catch was less important than the pursuit itself, plus the chance to relish the sights and sounds of our quarry's habitat—the bushes, beasties, and the sun-spangled waters themselves. Locked forever in memory are a multitude of vivid scenes of leaping fishes, bad casts taken by uncritical trout, morning steam rising from a river, deer poised in mid-drink at creekside, the pattern of light filtering through an old-growth forest canopy and dappling the trailside bracken. All these can be recalled at will and relished again and again.

Many of the favored haunts of past seasons have vanished at the hand of "progress"—urban development, our appetite for lumber, the ravages of erosion, and our continuing abuse of lands and watersheds. Yet some remain, and new places are still discovered now and then. Always, it seems, I can find somewhere to wet a line and take a fish or two, not in the sizes and quantities of past decades, but enough to keep casting skills from total rust, and enthusiasm for the outdoors from paling.

Fishwagons

I harbor fond memories of my grandfather's Model A Ford, probably the most dutiful fishing vehicle of its age (like me, past 60). Long before we were blessed with the specialty RV's now swooping the highways and back roads, the Model A fit the outdoorsman's needs and purse admirably. It could cruise the pavement, where available, at a breakneck 40 mph in reasonable comfort. It sat high and boxy, with road clearance to go over a sleeping sheep dog without disturbing a hair. And axle-deep mud was no obstacle. Gramp put nearly 200,000 miles on that sedan, in days when there weren't that many miles of road in all of Oregon and Washington, including logging roads and cow trails. Most of those miles were in quest of fish.

There were no Jeeps when I first did my own fish driving, and pickup trucks were strictly for the farm or commerce. I tried a few back-road jaunts in my father's Buick, but it was no great shakes beyond the pavement, where its long nose, housing a straight-8, shone best.

My first automotive investment (and by far the cheapest) was a neat 1934 Ford, reasonably abused by several owners before me, which fulfilled my immediate needs to impress girls and get me to and from, with luck, various fishing spots. It was red,

and had a large rusted hole in the muffler, which served nicely for both visual and audio effect. So much for the girls.

For fishing it might be described as adequate, if you discounted the springs—like tired rubber bands—and ground clearance capable only of surmounting pea gravel. It would go like a scalded owl, however, with a V-8 about the size powering today's lawn mowers. You could stuff in four fishermen of average size, all their fishing gear, plus foodstuffs and beer (six-packs were yet to be invented) for a week's sortie into the wilderness, and still have room for an always-needed extra gallon of gas. Only the very best of today's outdoor rigs can do as well.

Now I drive a big brute of a 4x4 pickup with a camper atop and a skiff atop that, and it will go just about anywhere I point it in semi-regal splendor, providing I buy out gas stations periodically, and check (again periodically—no, make that often) to see that its appetite for belts, hoses, sensors and little sealed boxes is filled. It is a fine, purposeful rig, indeed.

In between, I have owned a long list of used and new vehicles, all of them multi-purpose. I mean they had to be good at everything—carting lumber for house building and daughters to dances, playing commuter roulette and parking-lot bingo, vacationing the West and visiting the repair shop as seldom as possible. And, of course, fishing. They had to fish good.

From that lengthy list I might cite a few cars that did their fishing chores in one fashion or another:

1949 Ford "Woodie" station wagon. Huge capacity. Passenger-side door kept coming open on sharp corners, ejecting wife, other valuables. Got rid of when moss, mushrooms began thriving in woodwork. 60,000 miles.

1947 Studebaker flatbed truck. Very economical, would not start often. Great for hauling rockery boulders from secret alpine quarry. Would not get out of its own way on highway, but could low-gear it to Mount Rainier's summit, if asked. Only 6,000 miles (of mine) on this one.

1950 Hillman Minx. Britain has built some fine cars, but I forget which. This one could not long cope with American hills, dales, etc., even though nicely soldered together. Three clutches and out, I said.

1955 Ford station wagon. Probably the longest lasting of all, this well-shaped hunk of sheet iron withstood several crashes, overloads of house building materials, heaped invective from commuters, exposure to salt spray and other elements, and miles and miles of rutted, boulder-strewn, mudholed, and brush-lined logging trails. 140,000 miles.

1961 Lloydwagen. What, you never heard of a Lloydwagen? After the Volksbeetle, what could Germany do for an encore? This wasn't it. Two bicycles welded together, with an air-cooled, one-lung motorcycle engine up front, along with other working parts. A delightfuly tinny commuter, at 60 miles to the gallon, it could also negotiate narrow, rutted cow trails with pizzaz. Kept blowing pistons, however.

1964 Volksbeetle. I never really trusted this one, with its openly Teutonic arrogance and guttural exhaust. However, it would go many places where Jeeps feared to tread, sometimes on its side, or top, or even on its wheels if necessary. Splendid snow car, if you like snow.

1967 Chevy 3/4-ton pickup. A Chevy truck, need more be said? Solid, dutiful transportation. Plenty power, plenty noise. Hauls anything weighing 3/4 ton. Hauled big camper on this for 60,000 miles. Squirrel built nest on exhaust manifold. Fried squirrel.

1969 Chevy Van. First really one-shot type fishing rig. Built a rudimentary home inside: stove, sink, reefer, bunk, potty. Great for two well-acquainted fisher-folk. Many happy miles on this until fatal rust set in. Hand-painted band of fishes all the way around waist of vehicle, making same recognizable to fellow anglers and state troopers throughout the whole entire Northwest and other foreign and domestic areas.

1983 Ford 4x4 pickup. Possibly the last vehicle I will need to carry me and mine to fish spots here and also there, wherever that is. Quite a civilized way to go; refined plastic interior, with cute little jump seat in back for grandchildren and other extraneous equipment, neat map light for getting lost by, even air conditioning and tape deck. Under the hood, I presume, is a large and powerful horse, hidden beneath a canopy of hoses capable of plumbing a hydroelectric plant.

Fish Gods

Before you venture very far in the game of fly fishing you will become aware of the curious fact that there are elements beyond your control. Certain physical factors are in the hands of the gods, who are responsible for your success (or lack thereof), your comfort and enjoyment of the sport, regardless of your skill and enthusiasm.

Call it luck if you will, but your competence more often than not is governed by the actions of various gods. It's of no avail to pray, offer sacrifice or openly worship

these gods, but it is advisable to be aware of their presence and effect.

Even though fly fishing was not nearly as popular then as now, the ancient Greeks had gods whose functions covered all sorts of needs, desires, and sins—things like love, war, and sex. Some of these gods have faded to a degree over the centuries, but a number have survived to watch over various phases of sport. These include Humphrey, god of worm fishers; Circe, goddess of boulder-strewn waters; Demosthenes, god of pebbles in your wading shoes; Linus, god of floating fly lines; and Ernest, god of sink-tip lines, wind knots, and shooting heads.

Later on in history we begin to find saints of this and that, such as St. Hardy of the Impregnated Bamboo Rod, and St. Orvis of the Tackle Catalog. Later still other gods were invented to serve needs that didn't exist in the good old days of the ancient Greeks. For instance, there's Nicklaus, god of golfers; Jabbar, god of the slam dunk; Martena, goddess of the volley; and Toyota, god of four-wheel drives.

Try to stay on the good side of all of them.

Missing the Big Chance

The sun had slipped down below the canyon rim a thousand feet over my shoulder as I left the river and poked through the riverside brush to the dusty roadway. Chukars whistled from the talus slope and I heard a Jeep coming down the trail (a Jeep sounds like nothing but a jeep) and stepped aside as a dust cloud approached. A Jeep with a fancy canopy pulled alongside, and who should alight but Grits Gresham, well-known outdoor writer, television host, and beer-commercial celebrity. He was clad in a safari hat and grinning.

"Ah," I said, "leave the gate open, and anyone's liable to blow in."

"How's fishing?" he asked as the Grand Ronde murmured at our elbow. "Get any steelhead?"

"I raised a couple, but that's all," I said, determined to give away no secrets.

Grits said he and his buddy were mainly after chukars, but would love to get some photo footage of someone, namely me, hooking a steelhead. They offered a cold beer from their handy cooler and I was too overheated to refuse.

After draining the beer, I led them through the bushes, re-rigged, waded out to an appropriately photogenic spot, and cast to a piece of water where I had raised a fish earlier.

The camera turned. I cast and cast again, but nothing rose to my artfully presented fly.

"Guess they've gone to bed," Grits said as I waded ashore. "Nice try, nice casting, but I think we'll go chase chukars." With that, they Jeeped off down the road.

As the dust settled, I headed back through the bushes, waded out once more and, ignoring the failing light, put a long cast over a spot I knew surely held a fish. The drifting caddis disappeared in a purposeful bulge and I was fast to a good steelhead. Two jumps, and fish and fly went different directions.

"Yeah!" I hollered. And not a photo to show for it.

Thunder and Lightning

There we were, Steve Raymond and I, waist-deep in the Railroad Ranch reach of the Henry's Fork, casting to occasionally rising trout. A late afternoon streak of sun colored the sky to the west, and dark clouds massed overhead. Distant thunder rumbled. A few drops of rain spotted the river's surface.

We looked up at the first flickers of lightning, then at each other, shrugging. Both of us knew better than to be astream with our graphite lightning attractors. Yet we stayed, as the rain began in earnest. And the hatch commenced.

Where only a few mayflies had been around minutes before, the population suddenly swelled. Little Tricos, big green drakes, bigger whiskbroom-sized caddis. What a menu! And suddenly the trout were feasting, rolling and slurping with abandon as the thunder rolled.

I bent down, my eyes close to the surface, looking upstream to marvel at the oncoming winged armada.

"What fly in this competition?" I called to Steve.

"Give' em steak," he said, plopping a bushy caddis in front of a heavy bulge and promptly hooking a healthy rainbow.

The rain came on, peppering the river like birdshot. My yellow-bodied mayfly pattern was savaged time and again. Steve and I hooked a dozen each, fat rainbows and several browns, to three pounds.

Then the fishing suddenly turned off. Thunder symphonied in our ears. Rain drowned and frothed the river. Nearby lightning probed the sage flats. Only then did we splash ashore and head for the camper.

A Cathartic Expose of Why Fly-Fishing Books Never Make the Best-Seller List

It is interesting to note that very few books on fly fishing have been wildly successful outside the readership of active or potential fly fishers. This is predictably due to their lack of an underlying or dominant sex theme. Zillions of books deal with lust among princes and commoners, minorities, artists, entertainers, doctors, lawyers, politicians, advertising executives, hang-glider pilots, and small appliance repair persons, and all these sell like mad.

It is of course possible that the reading public (the book-buying portion) is compulsively tuned in to vicarious sex, while those into fly fishing are not. This I cannot believe. Yet few fishbooks, lacking heavy-breathing sex, make it to the best-seller lists.

To rectify this, and to keep you both awake and titillated, I have devoted this segment wholly to sex, and to hell with fly fishing, although I may drop a few sexy anecdotes or facts in succeeding chapters, if any.

Pardon My
BACKCAST

CHOOSING A FLY ROD

GENERAL PROCEDURES FOR SUCCESSFULLY FALLING IN

SAY IT WITH A SNEER

FISHFIGHTS

WHO INVENTED FLY FISHING

FLOATING CRAFT

MORE ABOUT CASTING

THE HIGHLY REGARDED DOUBLE-HAUL CAST

Alan Pratt

with illustrations by the author

11) Would you rather fish than (1) Lose your wife (2) Lose your job (3) Lose your virginity?

12) Do you lie (A) Always (B) Almost always (C) Only when mouth is open.

13) Do you drive a (1) Ford LTD (2) Aston-Martin (3) Hillman Minx (4) Rambler Station Wagon (5) Toyota 4x4 (6) Saab (7) Hudson Hornet (8) Harley Hog?

14) When your car quits, the first thing you check is (A) Catalytic converter (B) The garage door opener (C) Wheels.

15) Do you laugh at adversity (N) Always (3.2) Usually (ixv) Rarely.

The following questions are just questions:

16) Does your wife or companion know or approve of your fishing? (A) Yes. (B) No. (C) I have no companions.

17) Do you remember when a nickel would buy a candy bar or a cigar?

18) Can you field-strip an M-16 assault rifle? (A) Yes. (B) Why do you ask?

19) Have you read *The Decline and Fall of the Roman Empire*?

20) Can you locate on the globe: (A) Reykjavic (c) Cancun ($1.37) West Yellowstone?

21) Have you ever passed a post-dated check?

22) Do you react flatulently to (a) Beans (B) Chili (C) Asparagus?

23) Did you graduate from kindergarten?

24) Do you bat left, throw right?

25) Have you ever had (i) Acne (22) Gout (C) A lobotomy?

26) Do you bleed easily?

27) Do your children think you are God? (AA) Yes. (B) No. (T) Undecided.

28) Do you believe in (I) Acupuncture (16) Vitamin C (iii) God (4.61) Pedomancy?

29) Can you build a fire without a newspaper?

30) Can you program your VCR?

Frankly, there are no right or wrong answers. If you have the attention span shown by completing the quiz, you have what it takes to become a successful fly fisher.

Epilogue

I like trout fishing. I'm not obsessed, mind you, as my wife and kids insist, but nonetheless I would prefer to be on a stream or lake with a fly rod than doing something regularly regarded as productive. Not pretending to have encyclopedic knowledge of the sport, I still can boast of enough information to be comfortable among my peers, and enough of the argot of the game to hold up my end in a cocktail conversation.

Fortunately, I learned to fly fish early and have found it a great touchstone to my enjoyment of life, and to remaining somewhat sane in a rather insane world. If I have written and illustrated the game with seeming irreverence, forgive me, for I do so with deep affection, and the hope that, with humor and humility, you too may come to enjoy fly fishing as much as I do.

351 Words about the Author
(by the Author himself)

The reason for placing this splendid biography at the stern or rear of the book is self-evident; had you learned earlier these dreadful facts about the author you most likely would have lost your appetite and abandoned the whole entire project to the garbage compactor. Or, as his maternal grandfather on his mother's side once said, "Had I knowed I could of rode, I would of went." However.

ALAN PRATT, AKA Al Poltroon, or "Lucky Al," was born. Moments later, in 1922, Al and his alleged parents were driven out of Portland, Oregon (in a Model T) to settle near Alki Point in Seattle, where he learned to catch bullheads and shoot geoducks.

Al spent his youth skipping school and fishing, aiming for a career as a professional harmonica player or used-car salesman. Failing at these, he became a newspaper artist for *The Seattle Times* where, for 41 years, he was virtually a fixture, not unlike the plumbing or old Linotype machines. Drawing for the news, editorial, and feature pages, he was recognized far and also wide for his outdoor cartoons, especially the annual opening-day-of-the-trout season cartoons, which are now much prized.

Pratt has illustrated a dozen books, mostly on fishing, and with Milford Poltroon, publisher, put out the much-loved *Wretched Mess News*, a sort-of fishing periodical out of West Yellowstone, Montana, wherever that is. In his capacity as Litter & Pollution editor of the *Wretched Mess* he won many non-Pulitzer prizes, including a year's free parking in Rexburg, Idaho.

Al has taught fishing for the Fenwick Fly Fishing Schools, has fished or fallen into many of the famed waters of the West, as well as Canada, and even ventured to far New Zealand in quest of fish. Now retired, Al will continue to break rods, lose flies to bushes and perhaps fishes, repair leaky waders and visit new and old fishing holes. And maybe cartoon some.

Despite the fact that Al is only 6'2"* he has joined the Flat Earth Society, hopes to run for president as a Whig, and is well into his next book, titled "Creative Sloth."

*FINAL FOOTNOTE: Contrary to popular opinion, Al contains only 5 milligrams of baloney, plus less than 1/3 the sodium found in the average fisherman.